Mac Computer

Basics

For *Seniors*

- Mac OS 10.6 "Snow Leopard" Edition -

Michael Gorzka

Table of Contents

HOW TO USE THE APPLE MOUSE

New Mac computer users are often confused by Apple computer "mice" because they have only one button or (seemingly) no button at all:

The above picture shows the most recent Apple computer mice (at the time of this writing). Please keep in mind that you can use practically any computer mouse with your Apple computer.

Regardless of the type or model of Apple mouse that you have, here's how you can use it.

1) Move the mouse with your hand to place the tip of the screen arrow directly over the object that you want to click on (such as an icon on the "program dock"):

2) Hold the mouse very **still** as you press down --- and then quickly release --- the top part of the mouse:

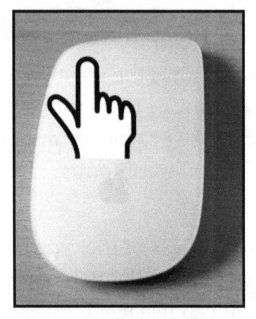

(The entire top part of the mouse is a mouse button.)

scroll button

If your Apple mouse has a scroll button (or wheel), you can use it (after some practice) to scroll up and down windows and web pages.

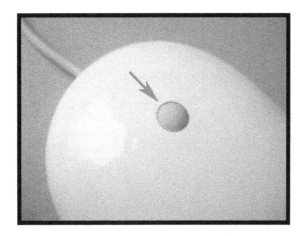

Pressing a scroll button (as opposed to *rolling* it) may automatically cause your dashboard widgets to appear:

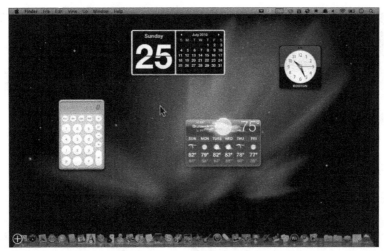

dashboard widgets

You can make the widgets go away by clicking on a blank area of the screen (i.e. anywhere off a widget) OR by holding down one of the "command" keys on your keyboard as you press the "tab" key:

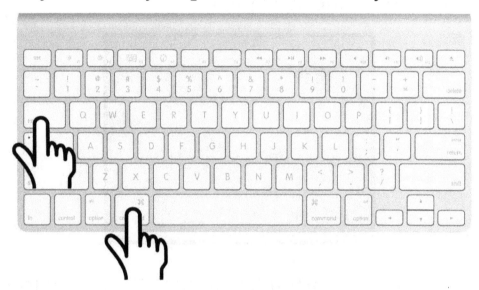

Pressing the "side buttons" on an Apple mouse may cause "Spaces" to appear:

We cover *Spaces* in "More Mac Computer Basics" but for right now, you can **quit** this application (and make your screen go back to a single item view) by pressing the "esc" key on your computer keyboard:

If the Apple mouse has only one button (or no button at all), how do I "right-mouse click"?

If you want a "pop-up menu" to appear (like the one circled on the next page), you can "control-click" the mouse.

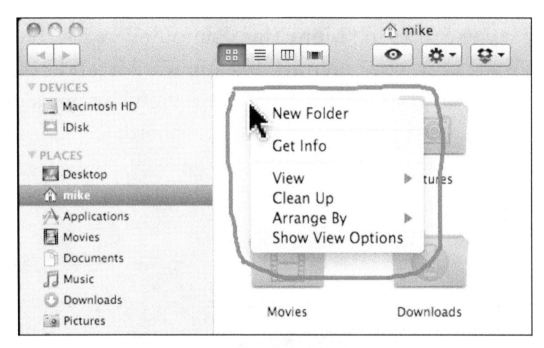

pop-up menu

"Control-clicking" the mouse entails **holding down** the "control" key on the bottom row of your keyboard as you click the mouse:

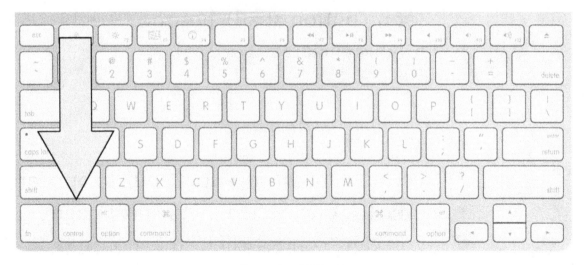

"control" key

After the pop-up menu appears, you can *release* the **control key** that you had been holding down and click *one time* on the desired menu selection:

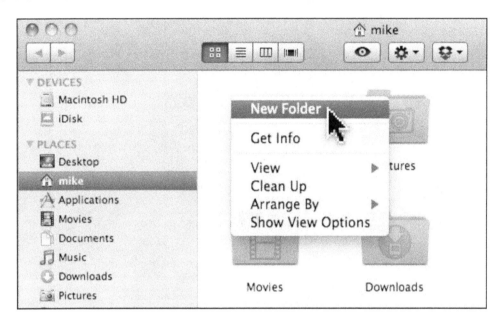

If you are coming from the *Windows* world and you prefer using a **two-button mouse**, you can use any **USB** mouse with your Mac (MacBook, iMac, Mac mini et al.)

Simply plug the end of the mouse cable into one of the USB "ports" on your Mac:

USB openings or "ports" are marked by this pitchfork like symbol:

(The above symbol will also be on the mouse cable.)

when to "double-click" the mouse

My beginning computer students often ask when they need to *double-click* the mouse.

The short answer to that question is "never".

Most of the item on your Mac computer screen (such as menu selections and the icons on your program dock) require only a **single-mouse click**.

To help avoid **Carpal Tunnel Syndrome** (and to prevent your Mac from working harder than it needs to) you should avoid unnecessary double-clicking.

You can (but you don't have to) *double-click* anything on the **right** side of a "Finder" window:

We'll discuss the "Finder" window in a later chapter.

For example, to start the "Chess" program from within a **Finder** window, you can use the mouse to place the tip of the screen arrow directly over that application (circled below):

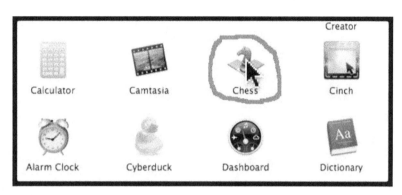

Hold the mouse very **still** as you press and release the mouse button *two times* in quick succession: knock knock!

The program will then start:

You can also double-click a **folder** (that is on the right side of a Finder window) to open it:

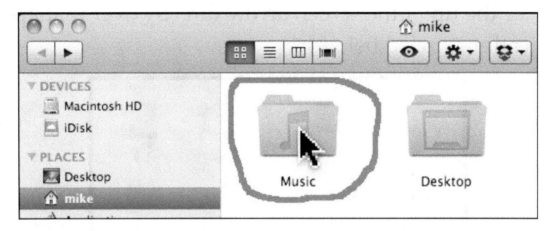

how to avoid double-clicking the mouse

As previously stated, you never **need** to double-click the mouse.

You could for example, click on an item *one time* (to *highlight* or select it):

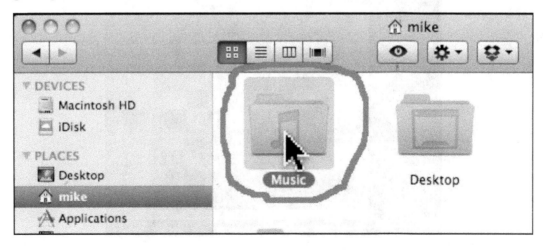

After the item is *selected,* you can then hold down one of the "command" keys as you type the letter "o":

command - o **keyboard shortcut**

You can start a program or open a **file** (such as a document or a photo) that is on your desktop the same way:

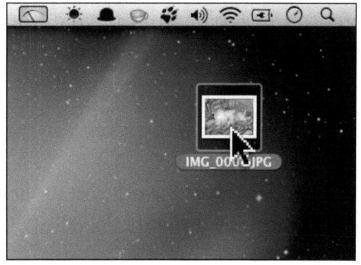

"mighty" and "magic" mice

Newer Apple computer mice have a great deal of functionality (beyond point and click) that can lead to some confusing situations.

You could for example, use the mouse to inadvertently "zoom" (i.e. **magnify**) a web page or cause your dashboard widgets to appear.

 We'll discuss how you can use the keyboard to **zoom** in and out in the "How to Use Your Apple Keyboard" chapter.

One could in fact devote an entire manual to the mouse that ships with new iMacs.

Until you get comfortable with the Mac, your author recommends that you keep your mouse use very **basic**:

1) Move the mouse to place the screen arrow.

2) "Click" the mouse to perform a certain action (i.e. start a program or make a menu selection).

HOW TO USE THE MACBOOK MOUSE

The *MacBook* (Apple's notebook computer) has a built-in computer mouse located below the keyboard:

Simply move your finger around the "Trackpad" to move the **screen arrow** (or "cursor") around your Mac's computer screen:

You can "click" the MacBook mouse by pressing down (and quickly releasing) the lower part of the Trackpad:

double-click

You can "double-click" the MacBook mouse by pressing and releasing the lower part of the trackpad two times in quick succession (knock knock!).

You can double-click anything on your desktop (or anything on the right side of a **Finder** window) but please single-click everything else.

pop-up menus

If you hold down the "control" key on your keyboard as you click the mouse...

"control-click"

... a pop-up menu will appear:

pop-up menu

The menu *selections* on the pop-up menu will **vary** depending on what the tip of the screen arrow is currently over.

HOW TO USE THE APPLE COMPUTER KEY-BOARD

Your Apple computer keyboard operates very much like a traditional typewriter:

There are some *differences* between the two though.

First of all, you don't have to press computer keys as **hard** as you would typewriter keys.

(Computer keyboards respond better to *gentle* tapping.)

Secondly, you can use the keyboard to *control your Mac* through its **function keys** and **keyboard shortcuts**.

function keys

At the very top of your Apple keyboard, you'll find a set of **function** keys:

You can press the **esc** key to "click" cancel buttons:

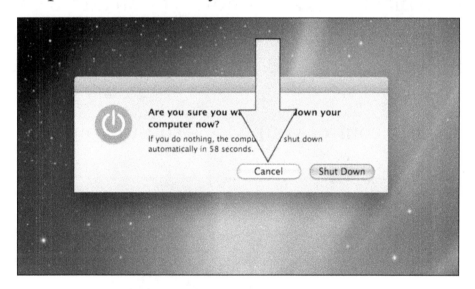

You can press the **F1** and **F2** keys to control the brightness of your Mac's screen:

You can press the **F3** and **F4** keys to activate (and **de-activate**) your dashboard widgets and "Spaces" application respectively.

The **F5** and **F6** keys (on some Apple keyboards) control the screen's *contrast*.

If you are playing a DVD (movie) or an audio CD, you can press the **F7**, **F8**, **F9** keys to rewind, pause / play, forward.

F10, **F11**, **F12** control your Mac's sound volume:

And finally, you can press the "eject" key to eject a CD, DVD, and/or software installation disc from your Mac (as long as the disc isn't being played or otherwise in use).

shift to create symbols

You can type a symbol (such as a % symbol or a **dollar sign**) by holding down one of the shift keys.

For example, to create the email address "at" symbol (@), you can **hold down** one of the shift keys as you press the key that has both the number 2 and the @ symbol on it:

return key

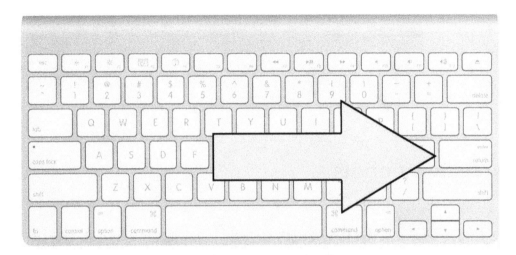

The "return" key can be a source of confusion due to the fact that it has multiple functions.

You can press the return key to "click" highlighted buttons on a window (circled below):

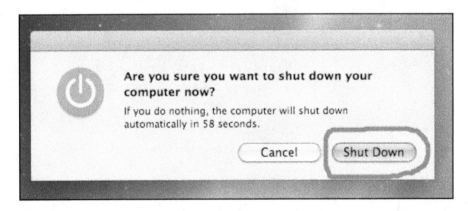

You can press the *return* key to move the "blinking line" (or text insertion point) **down** in an email message box or *TextEdit* document:

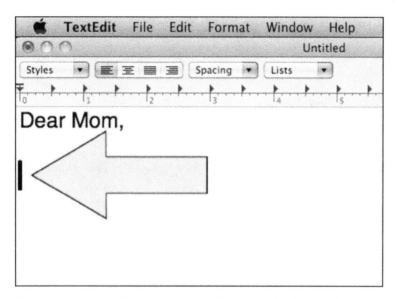

You can also press the *return* key to "click" a **Submit** or a **Sign in** button (pointed to below):

And (as we'll see in the "Surf the Web with Safari" chapter) you can press the *return key* **after** you type a web page's address (or URL) into the Safari web address box:

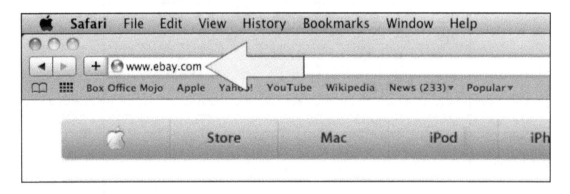

tab

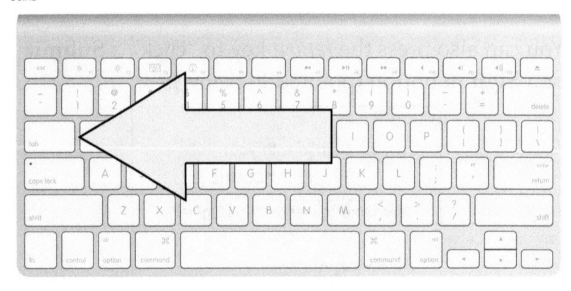

You can press the **tab** key to move the *text insertion point* (blinking line) to the next **tab stop** in a word processing document (just as you would with a typewriter) but you can also press the **tab** key to move the "blinking line" from one **text box** to the next:

delete key

The delete key is located near the upper right corner of the Apple computer keyboard:

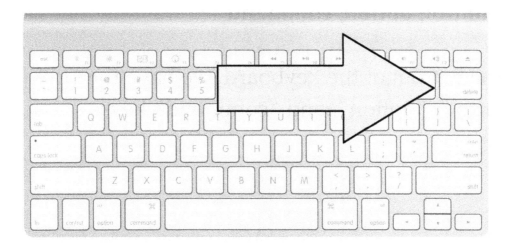

(The Apple *delete* key corresponds to the "backspace" key on a Windows computer keyboard and to the backspace key on a **typewriter**.)

You can press the delete key to erase text that is **left** of the *blinking line* (circled below):

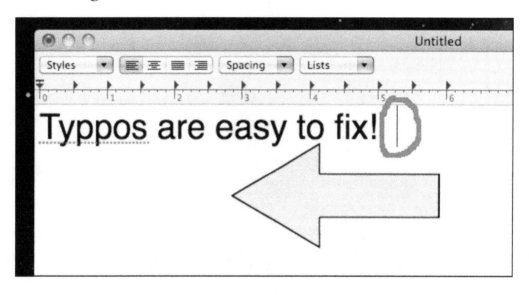

fn, control, option, command

At the bottom of the keyboard, we have the "fn", "control", "option", and "command" keys:

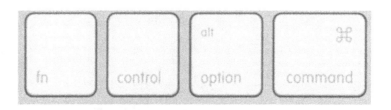

The **fn** key is found on MacBook keyboards.

You can hold it down as you are pressing the "delete" key to erase text that is to the **right** of the blinking line:

You can use this keyboard combination to do what the "delete" key does on a Windows computer keyboard.

The "control", "option", and "command" keys are used in various operations and keyboard shortcuts.

As we have already seen, you can hold down the "control" key --- as you click the mouse --- to cause a pop-up menu to appear:

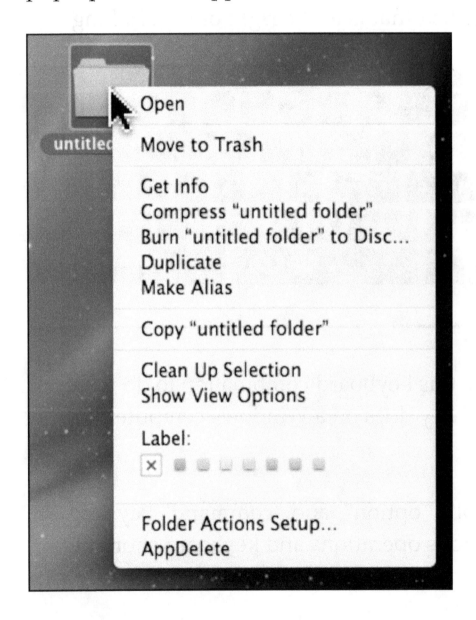

arrow keys

The *arrow* keys are located near the lower right corner of your keyboard:

As we'll see in upcoming chapters, you can press the arrow keys to *scroll* windows & web pages **and** to move the "blinking line" aka **text insertion point** around a document.

keyboard shortcuts

Due to provisions in the Americans with Disabilities act, any action that you can perform with a **computer mouse** (such as start a program or open a file) can also be performed with a keyboard.

This being the case, there are a *plethora* of keyboard shortcuts that you can use to make reaching for the mouse completely unnecessary.

For example, instead of using the mouse to select "Quit" from the iTunes menu...

...you can **quit** this application (or any other program on your Mac) by performing the "command-q" keyboard shortcut (i.e. hold down one of the "command" keys as you type the letter "q").

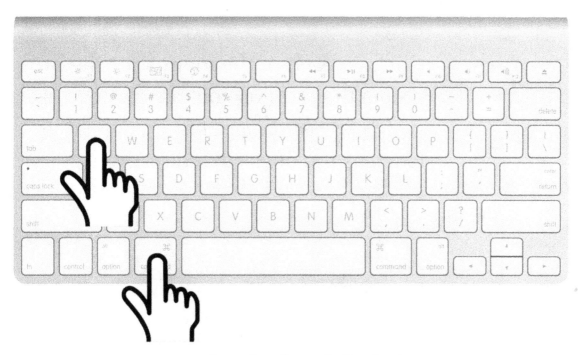

cmd + q keyboard shortcut

We'll see more keyboard shortcuts as we progress through this book and there's an entire chapter devoted to them in the video companion to this manual (available at www.mac-shy.com).

Click on each of the **menus** for the programs that you use on your Mac to see which *keyboard shortcuts* are available (such as the ones circled below):

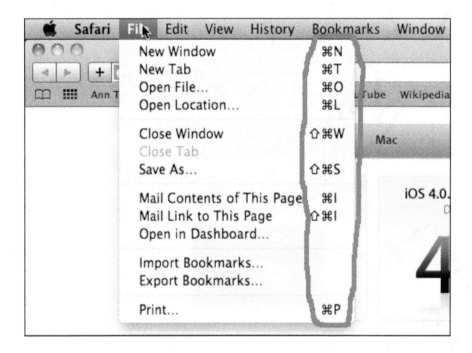

All of the keyboard shortcuts circled above involve the "command" key.

The upward pointing arrow in the "Mail Link to This Page" menu selection indicates that one of the keyboard **shift** keys must be held down in combination with the keyboard shortcut.

how to "zoom" in and out of web pages

If the text on a web page is too small for you to read, you can "zoom in" on the web page (which will **enlarge** the text and images on the web page) by *holding down* the command key on your keyboard as you press the key that has the plus (+) sign on it:

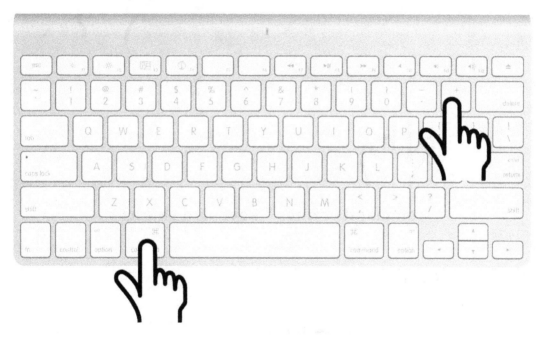

"command - plus" keyboard shortcut

Each time you perform the **"command - plus sign"** keyboard shortcut, the Web page will *zoom in* (and things will get bigger).

Conversely, you can zoom **out** of a web page (making the text and images *smaller*) by **holding down** one of the command keys as you press the minus sign:

"command - minus " keyboard shortcut

This functionality is also built into the MacBook trackpad:

It's unfortunately pretty easy to *accidentally / inadvertently* zoom in (or out) on a web page.

You can quickly restore the web page to its "default" size by holding down the command key as you type the zero key:

"command - zero " keyboard shortcut

You can also use the mouse to zoom in and out of web pages by clicking the Safari "View" menu.

please learn to type

I'm not saying you need to to be able to type 60 words per minute but really the "Hunt and Peck" method is for the birds (literally).

If you don't know how to (at least kinda sorta) type, you'll waste a lot of time and effort.

You'll want to spend your time exploring the capabilities of your Mac computer, getting things accomplished and having **fun** instead of hunting for keys on your keyboard.

As an **Adult Services Librarian** and computer technologies instructor, I quickly learned that it's very easy to inadvertently activate a **keyboard shortcut** if you're not fairly proficient with the computer keyboard.

(This fact caused a lot of stress, anxiety, and **lost work** amongst many of the library's public PC users.)

This being the case, practicing some keyboard exercises / activities will really pay off for you.

So my advice is if you can't type, please check a "How to Type" book out of your library…

1) Start the *TextEdit* program on your Mac by first holding down one of the "command" keys as you press the spacebar one time:

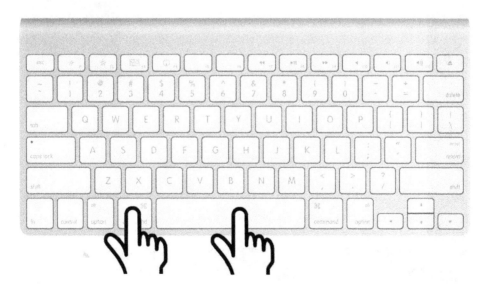

2) Type *textedit* into the **Spotlight** search box (which will appear at the top right corner of the screen):

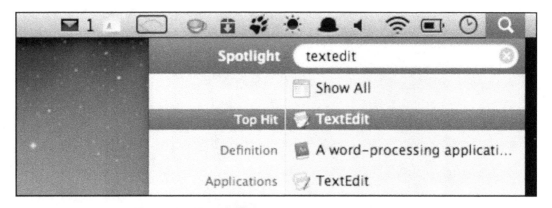

3) Press the "return" key on your keyboard.

The TextEdit program (or "application") will then start:

The "blinking line" will (by default) be at the top left corner of the TextEdit window (circled below):

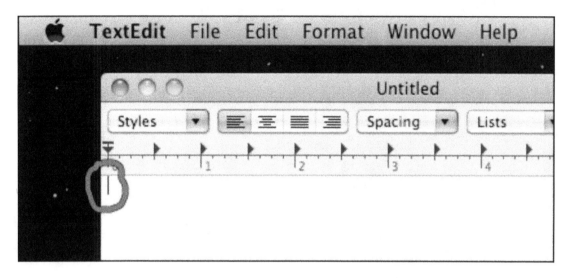

You can click the green "resize" button to make the TextEdit window take up your entire screen:

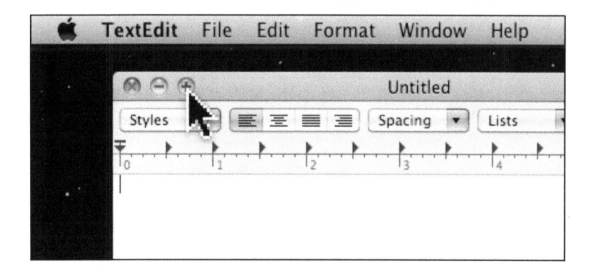

Next you can change the **text size** to something you can actually see by first holding down a "command" key as you press the letter "t" key:

"command - t" keyboard shortcut

This will cause the "Fonts" window to appear:

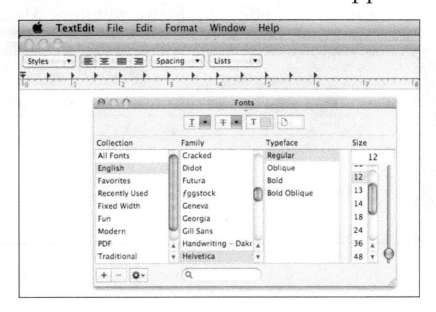

You can then use the mouse to select a larger text size (which is **36** in this example):

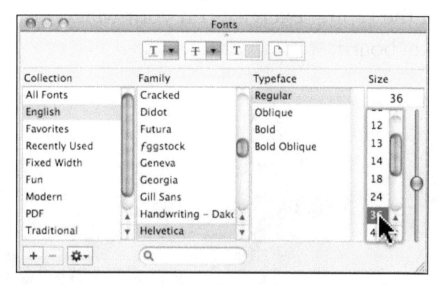

After you have selected a larger text size, you can **close** the *Fonts* window by clicking its red "close" button (circled below):

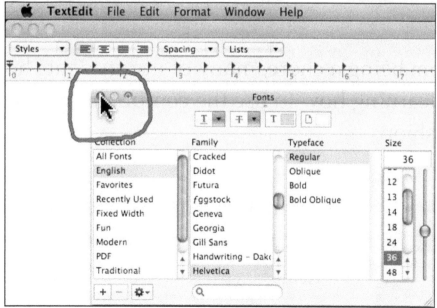

After you have started the *TextEdit* program; resized its window; and selected a larger text size; please **practice** the typing exercises on your MacBook or Apple keyboard:

Far from being a chore, many of my students have enjoyed learning how to use the computer keyboard in this fashion.

 We formally introduce the *TextEdit* application in a later chapter.

Again your only goals here are to be able to use both hands and all your fingers —- and to be able to look at the computer screen as you are typing.

Should I check out a "computer keyboarding" book?

Most (if not all) **computer keyboarding** books teach **Windows** computer keyboards — so to avoid confusion, I don't recommend them.

I learned how to type on an electric typewriter (way back in '82) and I made the transition to computer keyboards fairly easily (especially after getting hip to the special function keys and keyboard shortcuts).

The placement of letter keys on typewriters and computer keyboards is exactly the same.

MAC COMPUTER TOUR

In this chapter, we'll take a brief tour of your new Mac.

We'll cover each of the "places" that we visit here (such as how to open and empty your Mac's **Trash** can) in more detail as we progress through this book.

mac computer desktop

Your Mac computer "desktop" is so named because it's very similar (at least conceptually) to the top of an actual desk.

The Mac desktop has 3 main areas:

1) The menu bar (located at the top **left** corner of the screen):

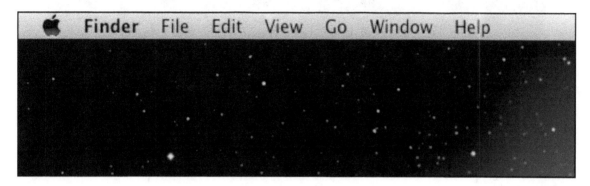

2) The menu bar applications area (top **right** corner of the screen):

3) The program dock (which by **default** will be at the bottom of your Mac's screen):

menus

The menus (and program name) will **change** depending on which program is currently *active*.

For example, if I started the **calculator** application, the top left corner of the screen would look like this:

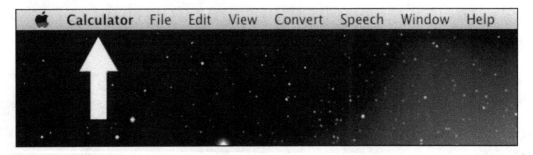

And here are the menus for the "Stickies" application:

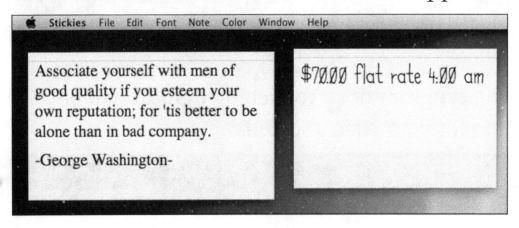

menu selection

You can click a menu one time to cause a "pull-down" menu to appear:

You can then *select* any of the items on the menu by clicking on it one time:

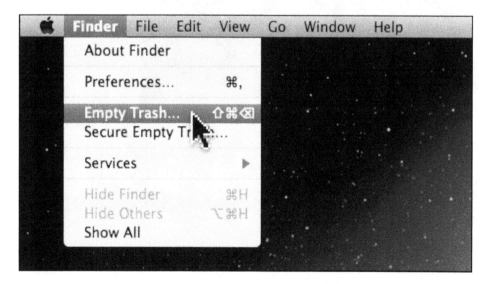

the "program dock"

Your Mac's "program dock" is split into two main areas.

Shortcut icons to various *programs* on your Mac will be on the left:

And **shortcuts** to your Mac's "Applications", "Documents" and "Downloads" folders will be on the right:

The program dock (like many things on your Mac) can be changed or *customized*.

Shortcut "icons" for both programs and folders can be **added** to your program dock and **removed** from it.

For example, if you often play the "Chess" game and would like easier access to it, you can add its shortcut **icon** to your program dock.

(We'll cover how to do that in the "How to Start & Quit Programs" chapter.)

trash can

And as we see here, you can also access your Mac's **Trash** from the program dock:

(You can "control-click" on the Trash to cause a *pop-up menu* to appear.)

menu bar

I have to admit that I love my menu bar applications!

They're convenient and offer some great functionality:

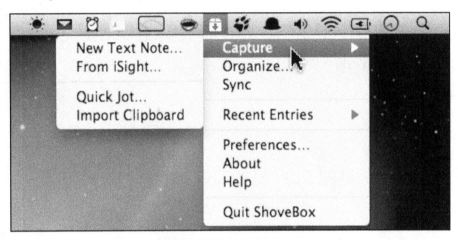

Menu bar apps also tend to be very **lightweight** in that they do not hog your Mac's processor nor do they gobble up a significant amount of memory:

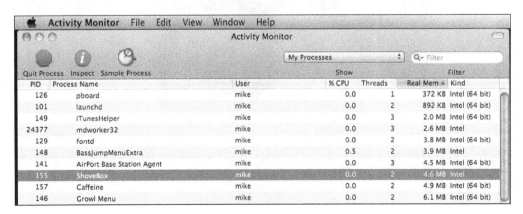

Some menu bar applications can be activated with the mouse:

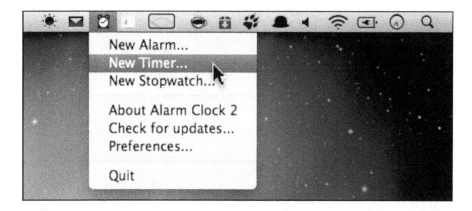

Many menu bar applications (such as **Alfred**) can be invoked with keyboard shortcuts:

For example, if I hold down the *option* key on my keyboard as I press the **spacebar**, the "Alfred" search window will appear:

I can then type in the *first few letters* of the name of the application that I wish to start:

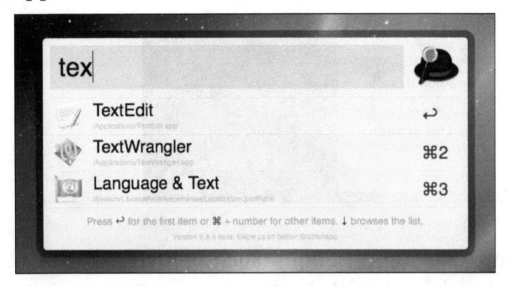

And then press the "return" key on my keyboard to start that program:

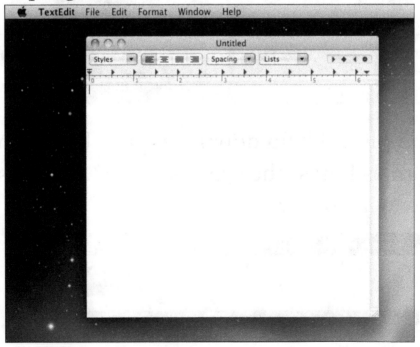

Other menu bar applications run in the *background* (e.g. "Growl") and *automatically* respond to your preferences:

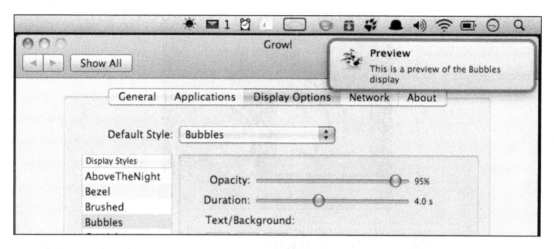

Growl is one of the most popular (and *free*) menu bar applications for the Mac.

We cover how to search for, download and **install** "Growl" (and other menu bar applications) in the *next* book in this series entitled "More Mac Computer Basics".

The menus that you'll see at the upper left side of the screen will **vary** depending on which program you are currently using (i.e. which program is currently **active**) but the menu bar applications will stay the same.

THE "FINDER" PROGRAM

Finder is the brains of your Mac computer.

It's the one program that will always be open:

You can *switch* to the Finder program (or make it **active**) by clicking its icon on the program dock (shown above) **or** by clicking anywhere on a *blank* area of your desktop (circled below):

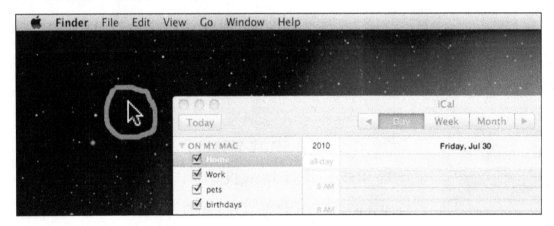

Please note that the iCal window is "grayed-out" in the above picture while *Finder* appears next to the .

For an *obstructed* view of your desktop, you can make **Finder** the active program and then select "Hide Others" from the Finder menu.

1) *Before* selecting "Hide Others":

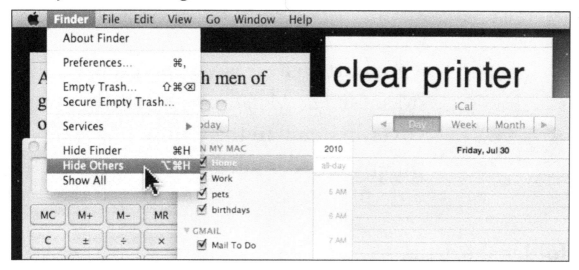

2) *After* selecting "Hide Others":

Why else would I want to *switch* to the Finder program?

The short answer is when you want to do some *File Management* (which we cover in detail in the "More Mac Computer Basics" book and instructional video).

folder shortcuts

Please note the *folder shortcuts* on the Finder "Go" menu:

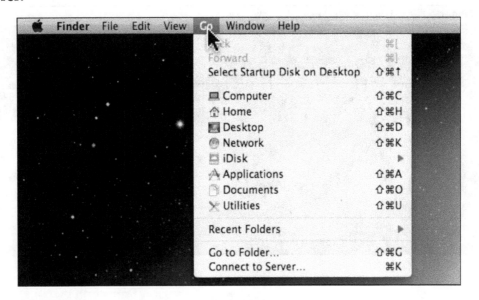

THE APPLE MENU

Regardless of which program is currently "active" on your Mac, you will see an apple (🍎) at the top left corner of your screen:

You can use the mouse to click this "apple" to cause a *pull-down* menu to appear:

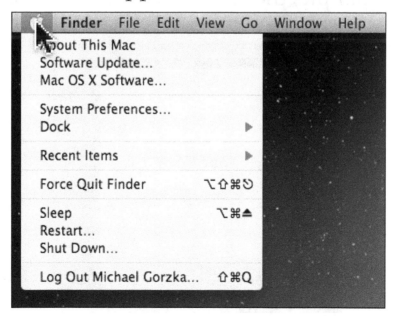

You can then *single-click* on the menu selection that you wish to make:

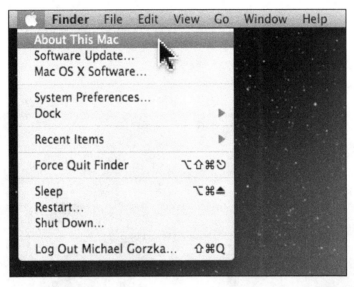

What happens next, depends on the menu selection that you just made.

Here for example, the "About This Mac" window appears:

You can select *Shut Down* from the menu...

...which will cause a "Shut Down" window to appear:

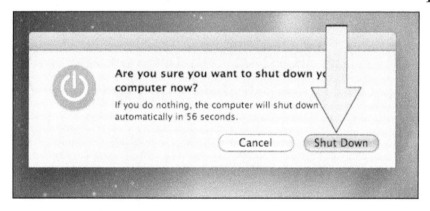

You can then either click the "Shut Down" button (pointed to above) or press the "return" key on your computer keyboard.

If you change your mind about shutting down your Mac, you can either click *Cancel* or press the *esc* key at the top left corner of your computer keyboard.

Restart

To restart your Mac, you can select "Restart" from the
 menu:

The "Restart" window works like the "Shut Down"
window.

You can click the "Restart" button (or press the *return*
key on your keyboard) to *immediately* restart your
Mac.

Or you can *cancel* (or abort) the **Restart** either by clicking the "Cancel" button or by pressing the "esc" key
at the top left corner of your keyboard.

If your Mac starts behaving *sluggishly*
(or stops operating as it should), try *re-
starting* your Mac before you call Apple
tech support.

Sleep

If you're not going to be using your Mac for a while, you can put it to "Sleep" in order to save energy and some **money** on your monthly utilities bill.

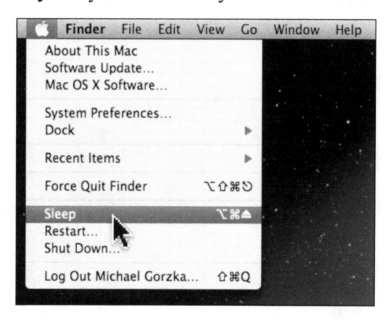

If you select "Sleep" from the Apple menu, your Mac will **immediately** go into a low power, energy-saving state (also called a "standby" mode) and your Mac's screen will go black.

To wake your Mac from "sleep" mode, you can either click the mouse or press any key on your Apple keyboard.

(We'll return to the Apple menu several more times as we progress through this book.)

THE FINDER WINDOW

The Finder window acts like a *doorway* into your Mac:

You can use it to access all of your Mac's applications, files and folders.

open a finder window

There are several ways you can open a Finder window on your Mac.

One way is to click the Finder "icon" on the far left side of the program dock:

This will make Finder the **active** program...

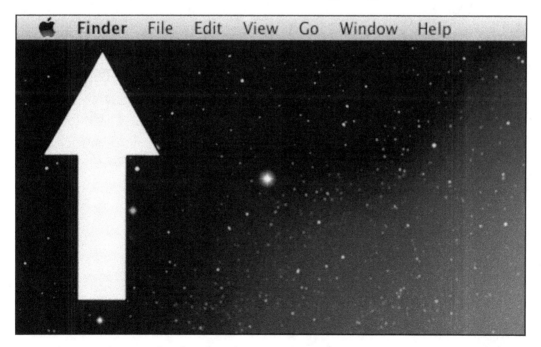

Finder is the "active" program

..and will also open a "Finder window":

close

You can close a "Finder window" by clicking its red "close" button at the top left corner of the window:

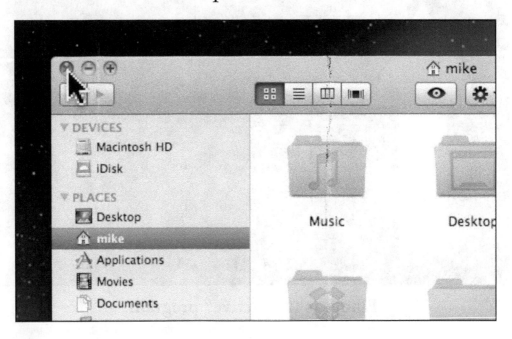

You can also hold down one of the "command" keys on your keyboard as you type the letter "w":

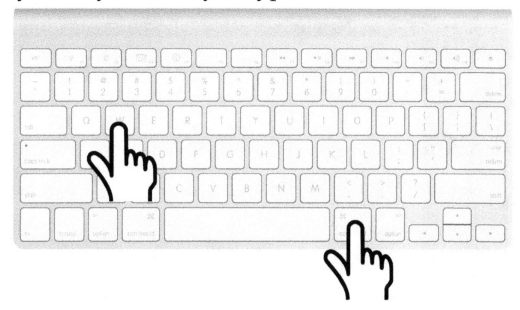

command - w keyboard shortcut

The "close" keyboard shortcut will close the window that is currently **active**.

This being the case you should make sure which window is currently <u>active</u> (i.e. has *colorful* buttons instead of "grayed-out buttons) **before** performing the "close" keyboard shortcut.

If (for example) you click anywhere outside the Finder window (circled below)...

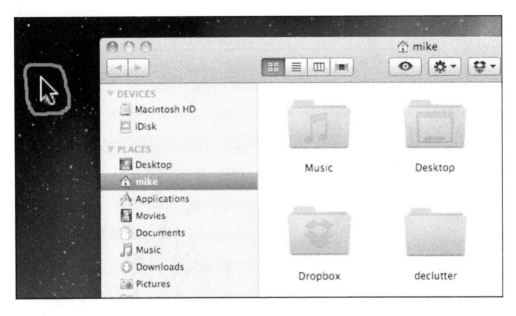

...the Finder window will become *grayed out* (i.e. inactive):

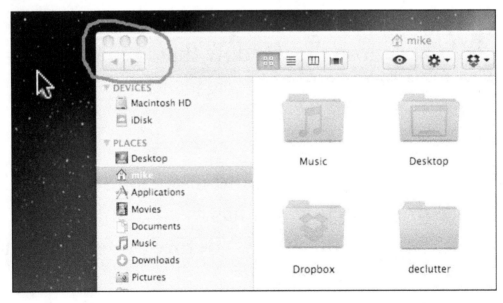

You can click anywhere on a window (circled below) to make it active:

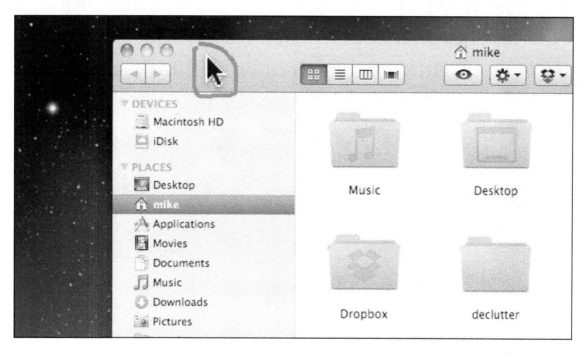

And then close it with the "command-w" keyboard shortcut.

My students often ask me what the "golden rule" is to learning how to use Mac computers.

My response is usually something like: "Take your time, stay organized, and know which **program** is active (or has *focus*) and which **window** is active."

minimize

You can move a Finder window (or any other window on your Mac) out of your way without actually *closing it* by clicking the window's yellow "minimize" button (circled below):

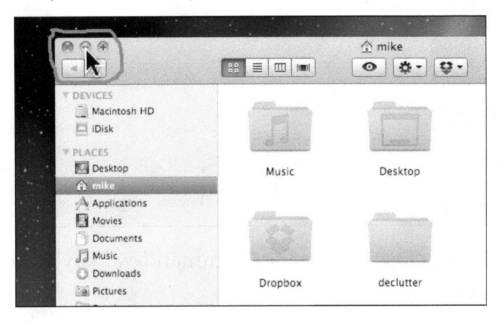

The *minimized* window will then appear next your Mac's trash:

You can get a *minimized* window back (i.e. make it regain its former size) by clicking its "thumbnail" near the lower right corner of the screen:

 Instead of clicking the *minimize* button, you can perform the "command - m" keyboard shortcut.

To minimize the active window in *slow motion*, you can hold down a **shift key** on your keyboard as you click the minimize button OR as you are performing the "command - m" keyboard shortcut.

Finder Window Tour

Near the top of the Finder window, you'll see the **name** of the folder that you are currently in:

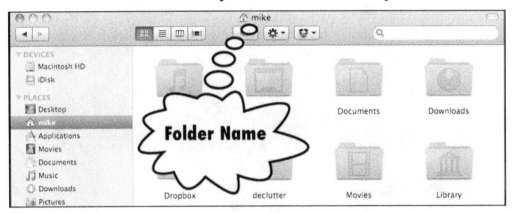

On the **left** side of the Finder window, you'll find a selection of "quick access" shortcuts:

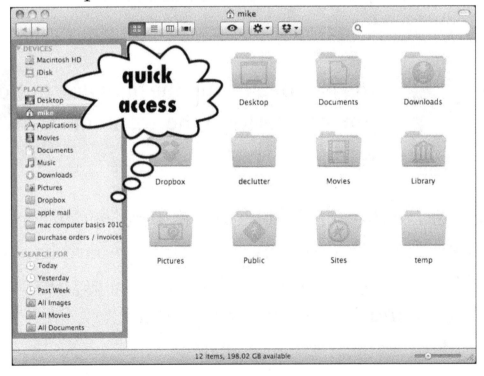

For example, you can open your Mac's "Applications" folder by *single-clicking* it within the "Places" section (circled below):

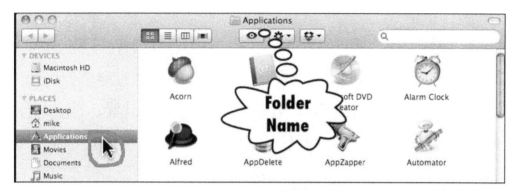

The **right** side of the Finder window will display the *contents* of the folder that you are in (e.g. the "Music" folder):

You can "double-click" anything on the **right** side of a Finder window to open it.

For example, to open the **iTunes** folder (which is *within* the **Music** folder), you can first use the mouse to place the tip of the screen directly over the folder (circled below):

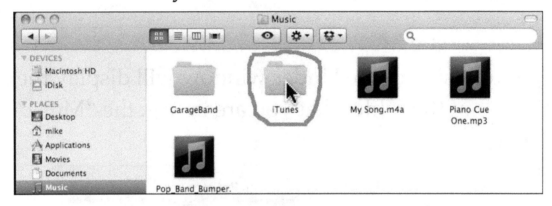

You could then press the mouse button *two times* in quick succession (knock knock):

You can also type the first letter(s) in a folder name to highlight or *select* that folder (circled below):

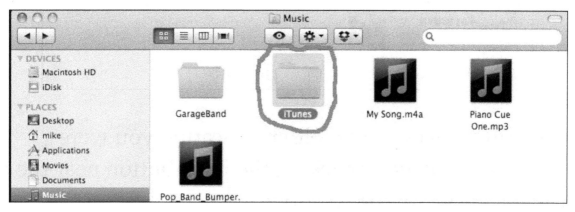

And then perform the "Open" keyboard shortcut:

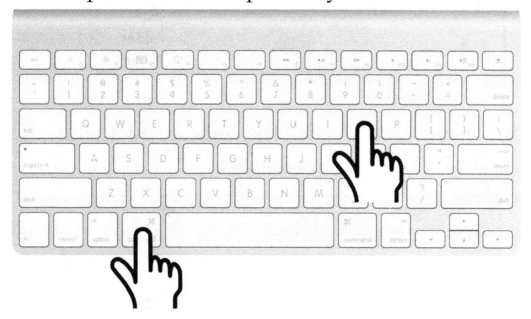

"command - o" keyboard shortcut

finder window navigation buttons

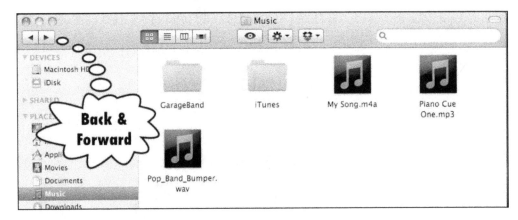

You can go back to the folder / location you were *most previously in* by clicking the **back** button near the top left corner of the window:

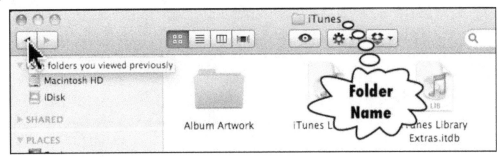

Conversely you can click the right arrow to move *forward* in your browsing history:

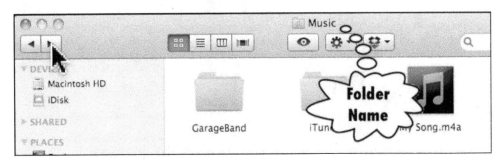

multiple finder windows

You can open *additional* Finder windows by using the mouse to select "New Finder Window" from the Finder **File** menu:

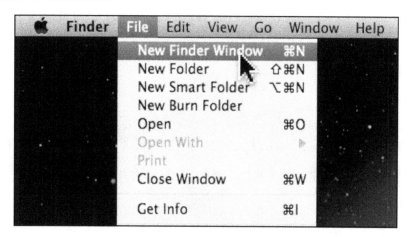

Each time you make this menu selection, a new **Finder** window will appear:

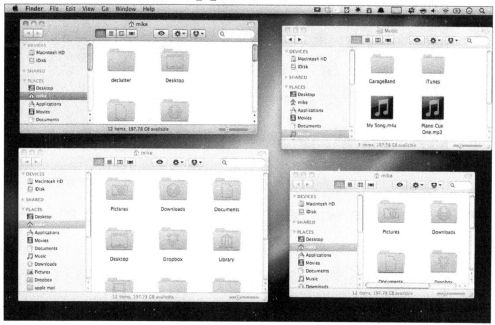

You can also open a Finder window by performing the "command - n" keyboard shortcut (i.e. **hold down** one of the "command" keys as you type the letter "n".)

Finder must be the *active* program on your Mac in order for this keyboard shortcut to cause a new Finder window to appear:

We will demonstrate ways to move files from one **folder** to another using two Finder windows in "More Mac Computer Basics".

places everyone, places!

As previously mentioned, you can *customize* your Mac environment to your liking.

In this section, we'll demonstrate how to add a shortcut to the **iTunes** folder to the "Places" section on the left side of the Finder window.

1) Open a **Finder** window (as previously described):

2) Open the "Music" folder either by *double-clicking* its folder icon in the **Home** folder (circled below) or by *single-clicking* its name or icon in the **Places** section (pointed to below):

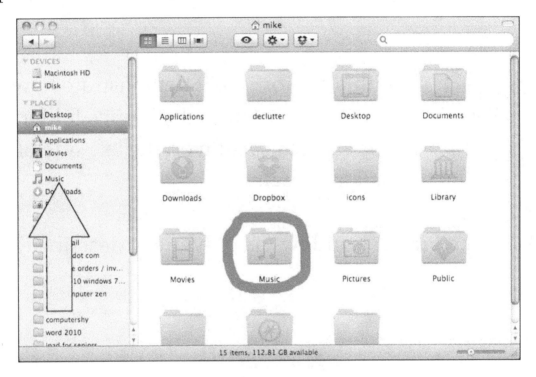

3) Use the mouse to place the tip of the screen arrow directly over the "iTunes" folder (circled below):

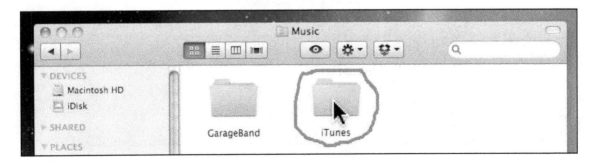

4) Press and hold down the mouse button --- and then *drag* the iTunes folder to where you want its shortcut to be in the "Places" section (circled below):

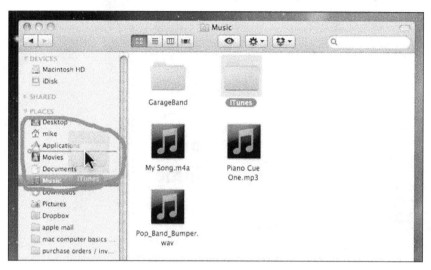

5) Release the mouse button that you had been holding down to **place** the shortcut (circled below):

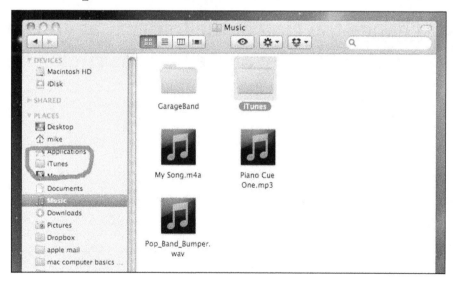

Now I can open the "iTunes" folder on my Mac (regardless of which folder I am currently in) by clicking one time on its shortcut within the "Places" section:

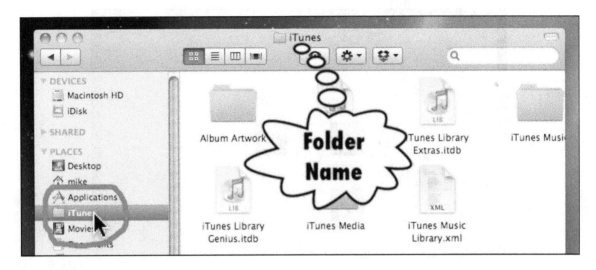

finder window "views"

You can change the *view* of the folder that you are currently in by clicking any of the buttons circled below:

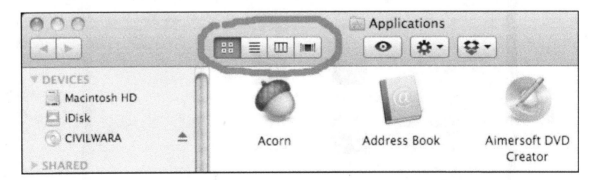

Currently we are in the "Icons" view.

Here we'll use the mouse to click the "list" view button:

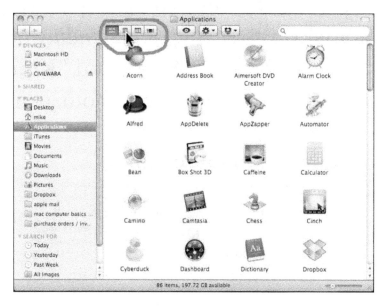

...which shows us the folder items in **list view** and also gives us a "Date Modified" column:

sort

While you're in "List" view, you can quickly **sort** the items in a folder (in *ascending* or *descending* order) by "Name", "Date Modified", "Size", and "**Kind**" (i.e. music, pdf, video, text document, photo, et al.).

Before clicking the "Name" column:

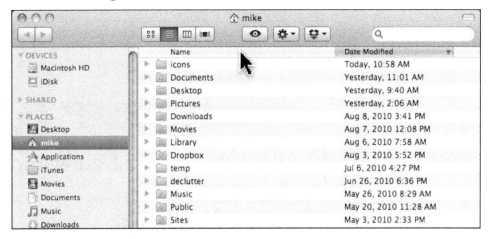

After clicking the "Name" column:

finder window preferences

By *default*, your Mac's "Home" folder will open when you first open a Finder window:

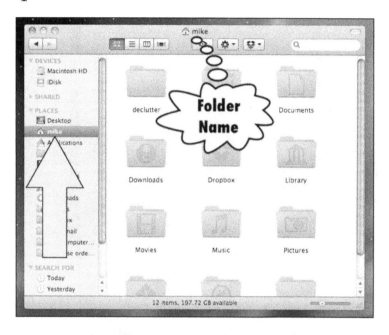

If you would rather have a *different* folder automatically open (such as your Mac's "Applications" folder), you can select "Preferences" from the **Finder** menu:

If necessary, click the **General** button and then click the "New Finder windows open" box (circled below):

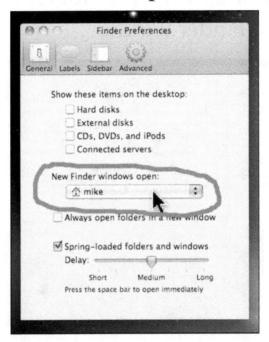

Select "Other..." from the pop-up menu:

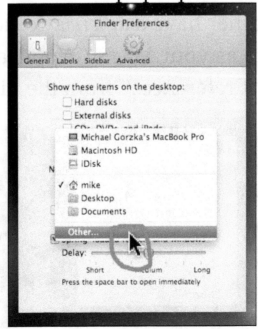

This will cause a *smaller* version of the **Finder** window to appear:

You can use the mouse to *select* a different folder:

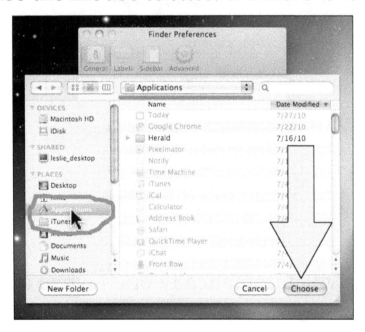

You can then click the **Choose** button (pointed to on the previous page) or press the "return" key on your keyboard.

This will place the folder that you selected in the "New Finder windows open" box:

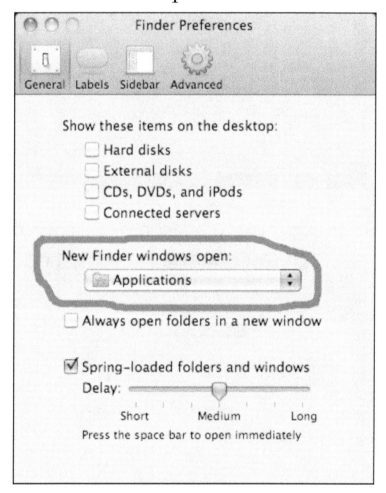

This folder will automatically open when a Finder window is summoned.

show these items on the desktop

You can click any of the "items" checkboxes to *display* that item on your desktop ("Hard disks" and "CDs, DVDs, and iPods" in this example):

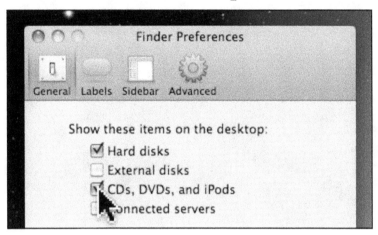

close preferences window

You can close the "Finder Preferences" window by clicking its **close** button:

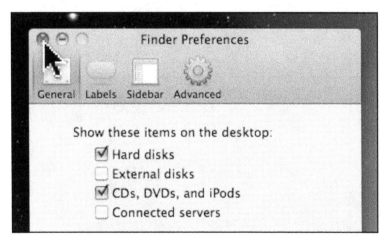

Here are the selected items on my desktop:

You can also open a **Finder window** by *double-clicking* the "Hard Disk" (Macintosh HD) icon:

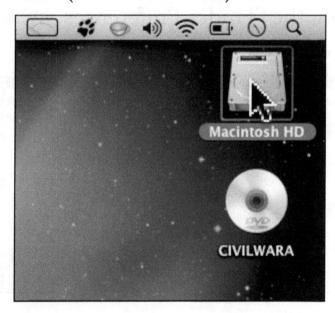

HOW TO START & QUIT PROGRAMS

You can start a program from your Mac's *program dock* by using the mouse to click its **icon** one time:

You can also start a program from within your Mac's Applications folder by first making **Finder** the active program (as previously described).

You can then click the **Finder** "Go" menu:

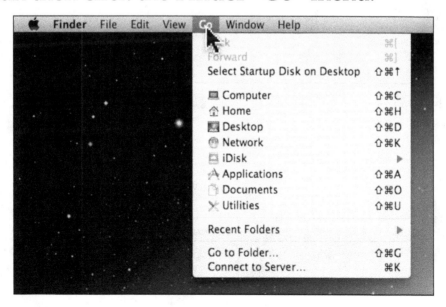

And then select "Applications":

The "Applications" folder will then open:

When **Finder** is active, you can quickly open the "Applications" folder by holding down *both* the shift and command keys as you press the letter "A" key:

"shift -command - A" keyboard shortcut

If necessary, **scroll up and down** the "Applications" folder (as described in the "Working with Mac Computer Windows" chapter):

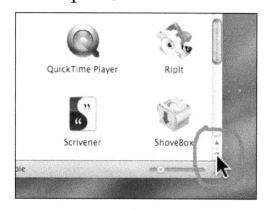

You can then use the mouse to *double-click* the program that you wish to start (circled below):

You can also click on the icon one time (to highlight or select it) and then perform the "open" keyboard shortcut:

start another program

You can start *another* program on your Mac by clicking its program dock icon:

Now **TextEdit** and **Address Book** are both open:

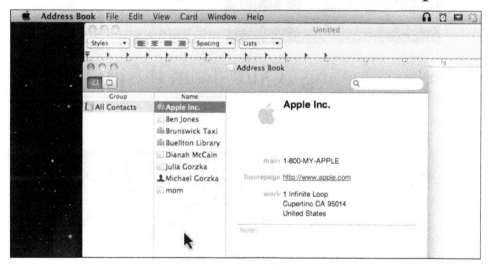

Please note that the TextEdit window (behind Address Book) is currently *inactive*.

You can also make **Finder** the active program and then start another program from within your Mac's "Applications" folder (as previously described).

quit a program

You can "quit" a program by first clicking the program name (at the top left corner of the **screen**):

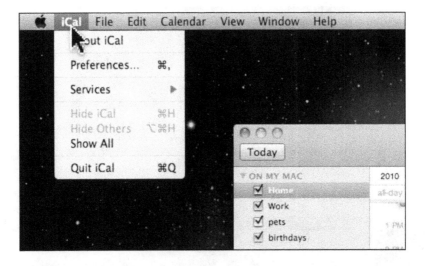

And then by selecting "Quit" from the pull-down menu:

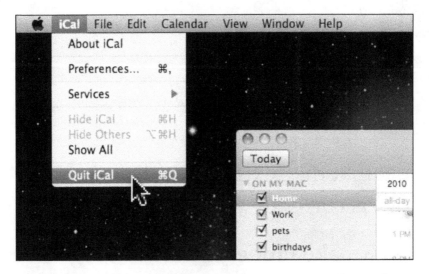

(Please note the "command - q" keyboard shortcut on the **quit** menu selection.)

force quit

If an application "freezes" on you and refuses to *quit*, you can select **Force Quit** from the menu:

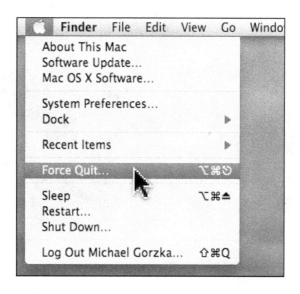

You can then select the "frozen" application and press the *return* key on your computer keyboard:

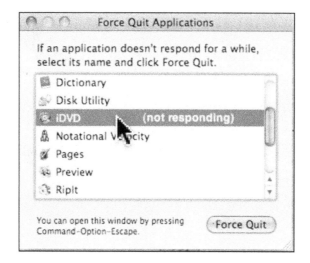

HOW TO SWITCH BETWEEN OPEN PROGRAMS

You can **switch** to another program that you currently have open by clicking its icon on the program dock:

What if I started the program from within the "Applications" folder?

All open programs will have an icon on the program dock.

If you start a program on your Mac that does **not** have a **permanent** icon on the program dock, a *temporary* icon for that program will appear on the right side:

How do I add a **permanent** shortcut icon to the program dock?

You can "control-click" a *temporary* icon and select "Keep in Dock" from the pop-up menu.

1) Start the program from within the *Applications* folder or by using *Spotlight*.

2) Hold down the "control" key on your computer keyboard and click the temporary icon:

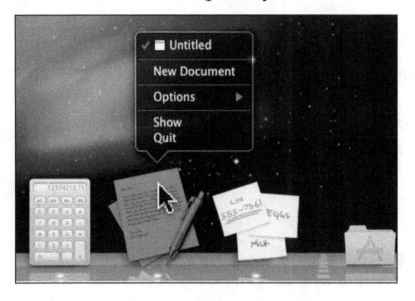

3) *Release* the control key you had been holding down and place the tip of your screen arrow over *Options*:

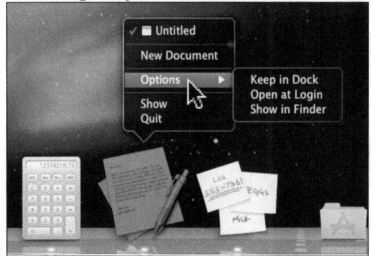

4) Select "Keep in Dock" from the *Options* sub-menu:

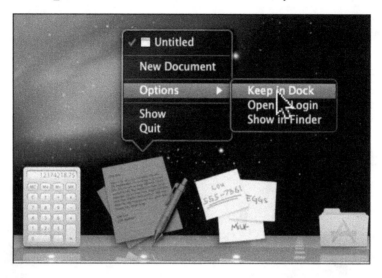

5) You can **hold down** the mouse button and "drag" the icon to where you want it to be on the dock:

(You actually don't have to *control-click* on a temporary dock icon. If you drag it to another location on the program dock, it will stay there permanently.)

switch programs by clicking on a program window

You can **switch** programs by clicking *anywhere* on the window of the program you wish to switch to.

Before mouse click (circled below):

After mouse click (circled below):

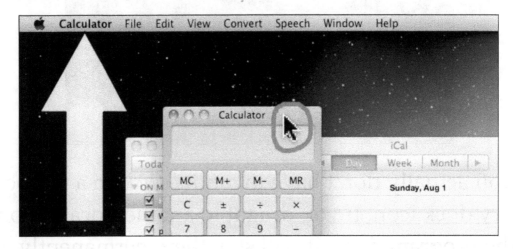

You can **hide** all windows —- except the window that is current **active** by selecting "Hide Others" from the program menu:

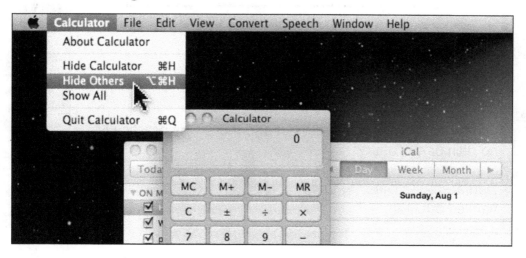

Please note the "option-command-h" *keyboard shortcut* on the "Hide Others" menu selection.

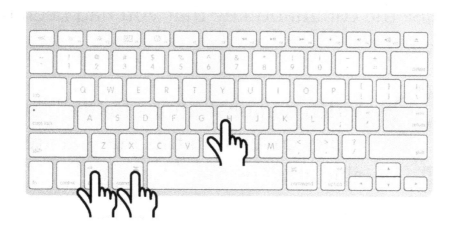

option-command-h keyboard shortcut

command-tab

A faster way to switch from one program to another is to **hold down** the "command" key on your Apple computer keyboard as you press the "tab" key:

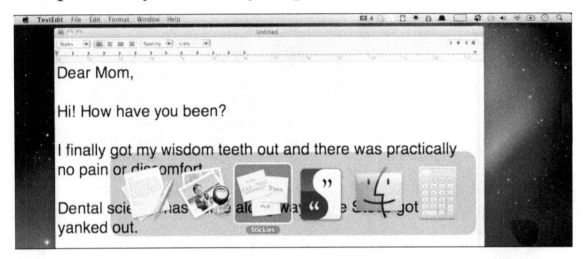

When the program that you wish to switch to is high-lighted (as *Stickies* is above), stop pressing the tab key and *release* the command key that you had been hold-ing down.

Video demonstrations for each of the topics covered in this manual are available at www.mac-shy.com.

WORKING WITH MAC COMPUTER WINDOWS

Many of the windows on your Mac will have three buttons at the top left corner:

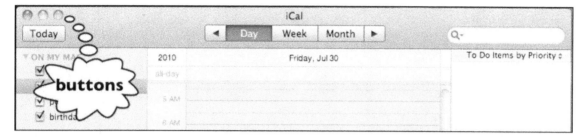

resize window

Clicking the green *resize* button will cause the window to automatically expand or contract (depending on the items inside the window).

Before auto-resize:

After auto-resize:

close button

You can close a window by clicking its red *close* button (circled below):

Closing an application's *window(s)* may not "quit" the program.

This can be a source of confusion for new and veteran Mac computer users.

Here for example, the *Preview* window has been **closed** but the application itself is still running:

If you *quit* a program, all the windows for that program will **close**.

(Although you may be prompted to **save** any changes you made to a file.)

A program can have more than one window open.

Here for example, I have three *Preview* windows open (each containing a different photo):

minimize

You can *minimize* an *application* window just as you can a "Finder window" (as outlined in that chapter).

Before minimize (screen arrow circled):

After minimize:

Please note in the above picture that the *Preview* window is visible even though *Calculator* is still the **active** program.

how to "manually" resize a window

First use the mouse to place the **tip** of the screen arrow directly over the *lower right corner* of the window:

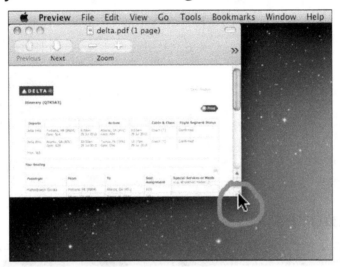

Press & **hold down** the mouse button and then move the mouse with your hand to resize the window:

If you are using a MacBook, you can press and *hold down* the mouse button with one finger as you use another finger to resize the window:

move windows

1) Use the mouse to place the tip of your screen arrow anywhere over the window bar (circled below):

2) Press and **hold down** the mouse button and move the mouse with your hand to move the window.

3) When the window is where you want it to be, you can stop moving the mouse with your hand and *release* the mouse button you had been holding down:

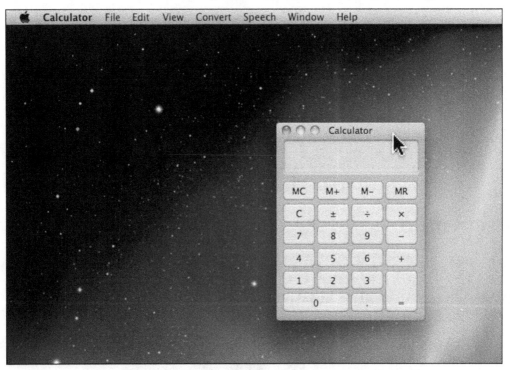

If a window is filling up your entire computer screen, you can click the green "resize" button to make the window smaller.

If you are using a MacBook mouse, you can press and **hold down** the mouse button with one finger and use *another* finger to move the window:

Using the built-in MacBook mouse takes a bit of practice but it will soon become easy and intuitive.

Please also remember that you can use a desktop mouse with your MacBook.

window scrolling

You can *scroll* up and down a window by using the mouse to move the **vertical scrollbar** on the right side of the window (circled below):

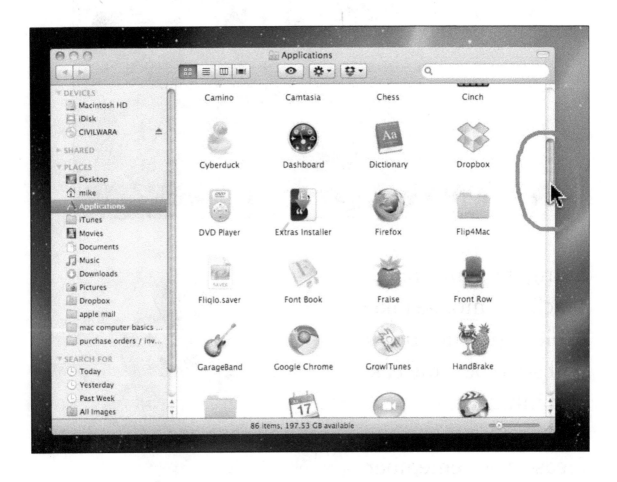

(You must **hold down** the mouse button to move the scrollbar.)

You can also press the **arrow** keys near the lower right corner of your keyboard to *scroll* a window:

If a window *doesn't* scroll when you press the arrow keys, you can first use the mouse to click on a blank area of the window:

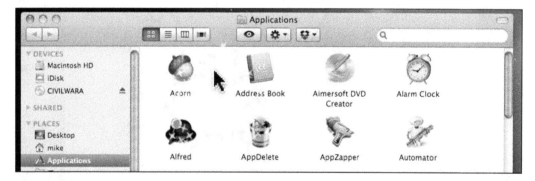

You can *then* press the arrow keys to scroll the window (from **side to side** as well as **up and down**).

If a **horizontal** scroll bar appears at the bottom of the window, you can press the *left and right arrow keys* to scroll the window from **side to side**.

Or you can click the green "resize" button:

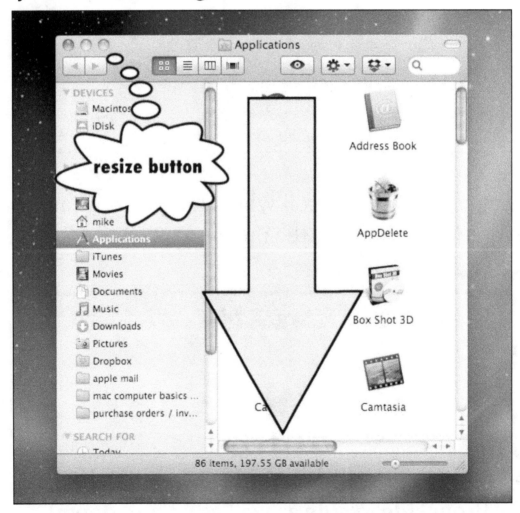

HOW TO CREATE AND SAVE A DOCUMENT

start textedit

1) You can start your Mac's **TextEdit** application by first (if necessary) opening a Finder window:

Clicking the "Finder" icon on your program dock will make Finder the **active** program on your Mac and will also open a Finder window.

2) Open the "Applications" folder by *single-clicking* it on the left side of the Finder window (circled below):

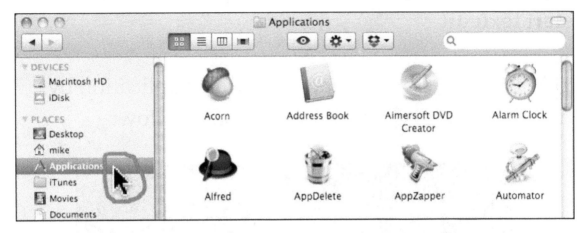

3) Scroll down the window until you see the "TextEdit" application (circled below):

4) You can then *double-click* the application to start it:

Perform the "option - command - h" keyboard short-cut to **hide** the *inactive* windows:

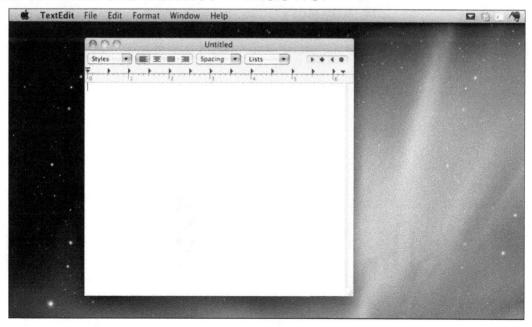

You can **resize** windows on your Mac and **move them** around the screen (as described in the previous chapter).

textedit preferences

The *default* text sizes are pretty small (especially for your author's baby boomer peepers).

This being the case (with TextEdit being **active**), we'll summon the TextEdit "Preferences" window with the *command - comma* keyboard shortcut:

If necessary, click the "New Document" tab near the top of the Preferences window:

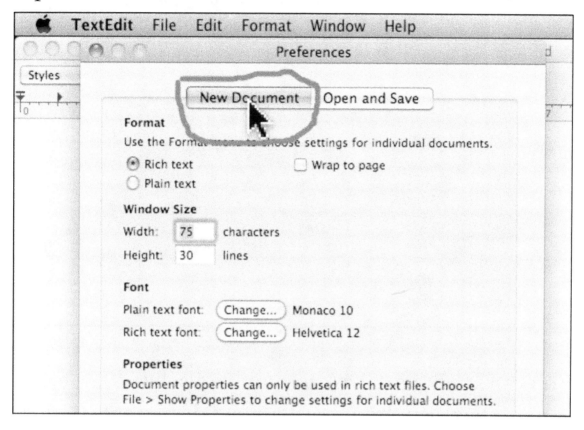

Click the "Change…" button for **Plain text font**….

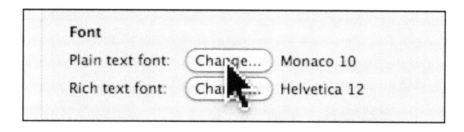

("Plain text" documents are unformatted.)

...which will cause a "Fonts" window to appear:

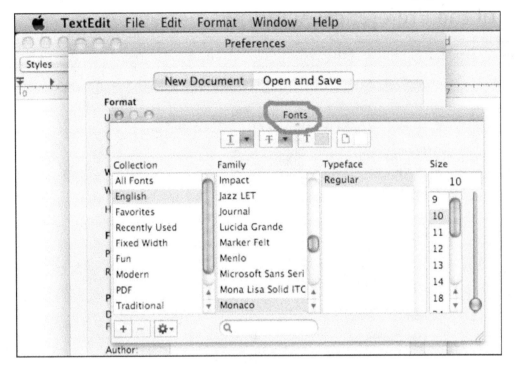

You can *scroll* the "Size" column and select a larger **default** text size for your plain text documents (which in this example with be **18**):

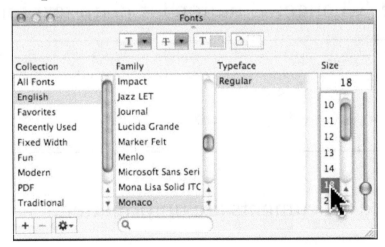

You can then close the "Fonts" window by clicking its red "close" button (circled below):

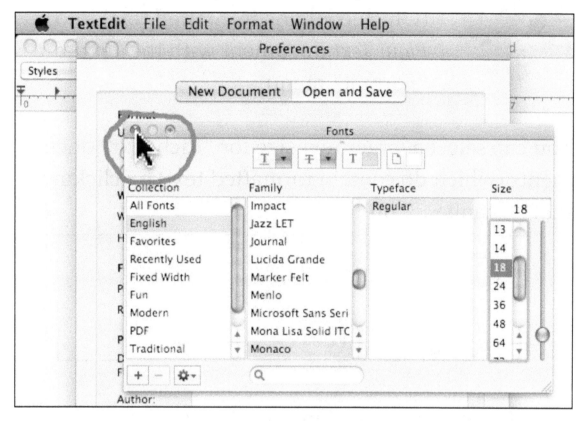

Please note that the text size that we just selected is now the **default** size for *plain text* documents:

 You can *convert* a "Rich Text" document (which contains **formatted text**) into a *Plain Text* document with the TextEdit "Format" menu.

You can select a larger text size for "Rich text" documents (which **do** contain formatted text) by clicking that "Change..." button:

Here I've selected the "Optima" font (as I prefer it to Helvetica) and typed "20" into the *Size* box:

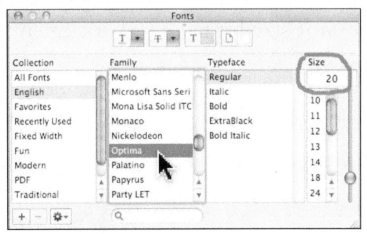

Finally, we'll close the TextEdit "Preferences" window (circled below):

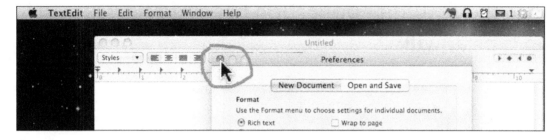

Please note that we have only set the **default** text size and font family.

You can select *different* text sizes and font families for individual documents:

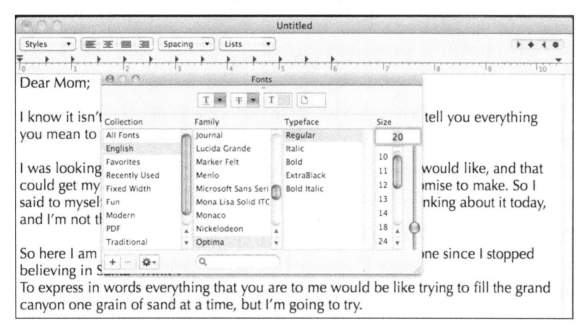

You can summon the *Fonts* window (shown above) with the "command - t" keyboard shortcut.

create a document

Once the TextEdit application has been started, you can type at will:

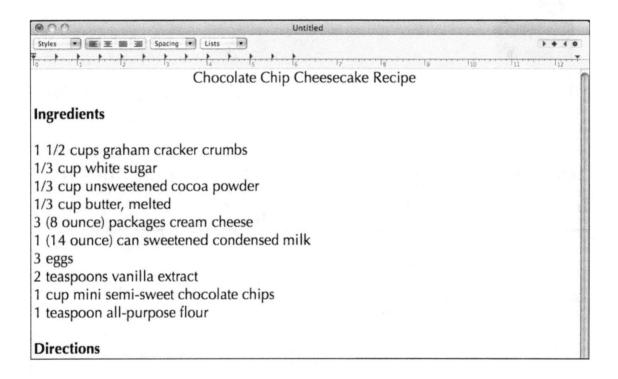

 We cover **word processing** in much more detail in "Word Processing Made Easy: a-step-by-step guide for mac computer users".

save a document

You can *save* a document either by selecting "Save" from the TextEdit **File** menu...

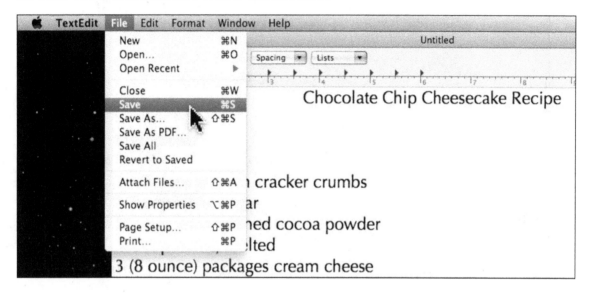

.... or with the "command + s" keyboard shortcut:

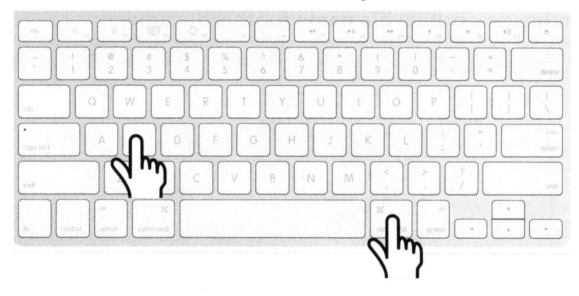

the "save as" window

The **first** time you save a document, a "save as" window will appear:

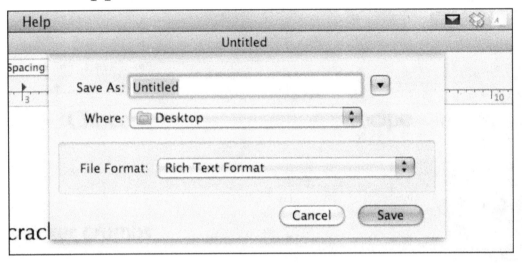

Please note that the "Save As:" box is *highlighted*.

This being the case, we can go ahead and type in a more descriptive **file name** for this document:

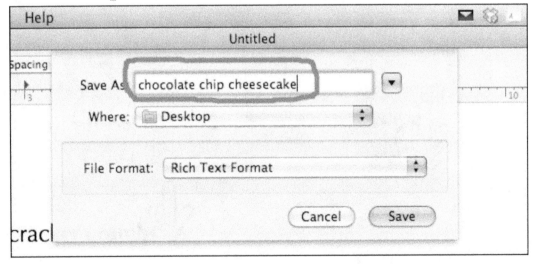

We want to save this document into the "Documents" folder on this Mac, so we'll click the "Where" box…

… and select "Documents" from the **Where** menu:

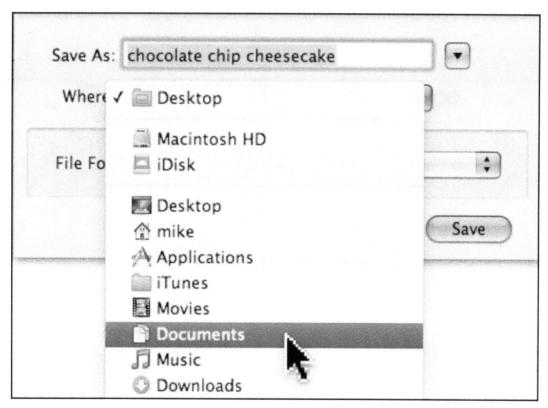

Finally, after **naming** the document and selecting a **folder** for it, we can either click the "Save" button (or press the keyboard **return** key):

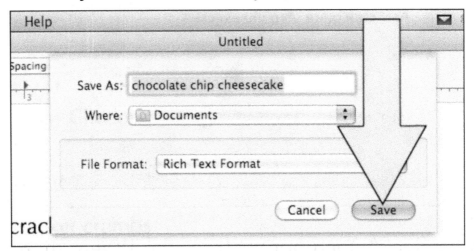

quit textedit

After you have **saved** your work, you can exit or "quit" the TextEdit application by selecting "Quit" from the TextEdit menu:

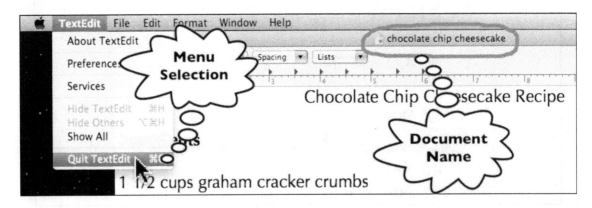

OPEN A DOCUMENT (OR A "FILE")

There are *numerous* ways you can open a document (or any other **file**) on your Mac.

Perhaps the fastest way is with *Spotlight* (which we also used to open the TextEdit application in the "Apple Keyboard Intro" chapter).

We'll begin by clicking the "magnifying glass" at the top right corner of the screen:

(You can also summon the *Spotlight* search box with the "command - spacebar" keyboard shortcut.)

Next we'll type the **file name** of the document that we're looking for (or words that we know are somewhere in that document):

If necessary, you can press the **arrow keys** on your keyboard to highlight the file that you wish to open (as shown above) and then press the **return** key on your keyboard.

The file (whatever it is) will then open:

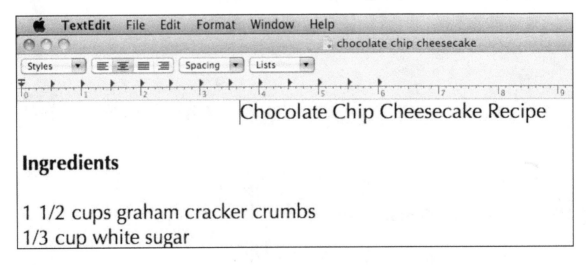

"recent items"

If the document that you seek is one that you recently had open, you can use the Apple menu's "Recent Items" menu selection.

1) Click the :

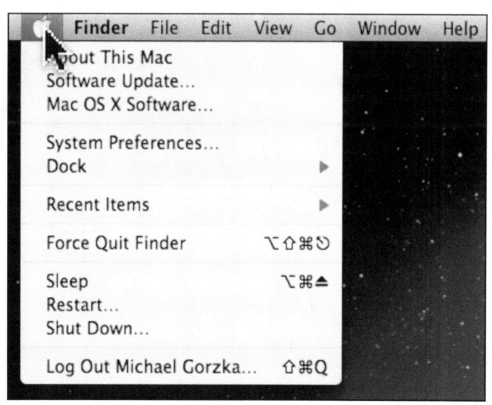

2) Place the tip of your screen arrow over **Recent Items**:

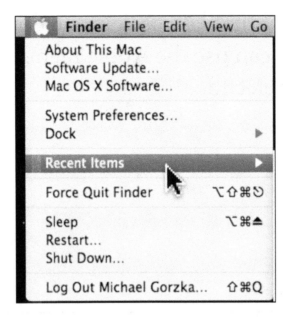

3) Single-click the file that you wish to open:

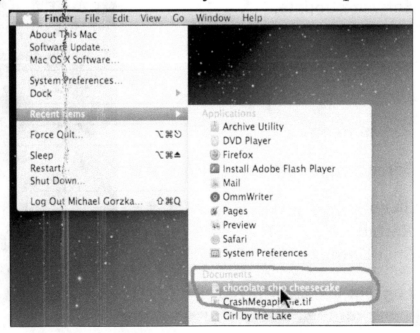

TAKE OUT THE PAPERS AND TRASH

You can *delete* a file or a folder on your Mac by first clicking on it *one time* to highlight or select it:

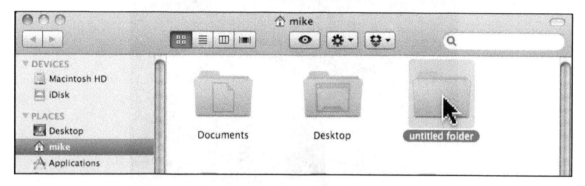

You can then hold down one of the "command" keys on your keyboard as you press the delete key:

command - delete keyboard shortcut

The selected file(s) will then be thrown into your Mac's Trash:

empty your mac's trash can

Anything you throw into your Mac's *trash can* will remain there (taking up space on your Mac's hard drive) until you *empty* the trash.

Make Finder the active program (as previously described).

Select "Empty Trash" from the **Finder** menu:

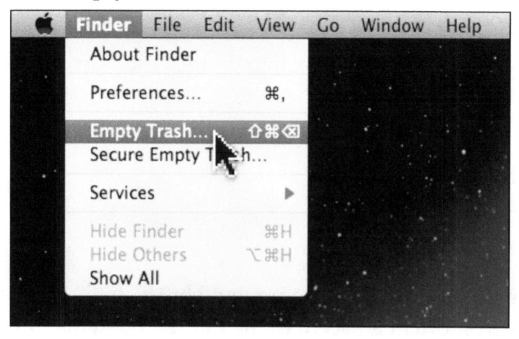

This will cause an "Are you sure you want to **permanently** erase the items in the Trash" message to appear:

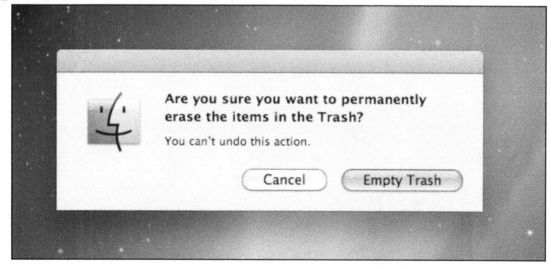

If you *are* sure, you can press the **return** key on your keyboard.

If you're *not* sure, you can press the "esc" key on your keyboard instead (or click the "Cancel" button).

Please note the nifty "command-shift-delete" keyboard shortcut adjacent to the **Empty Trash** menu selection:

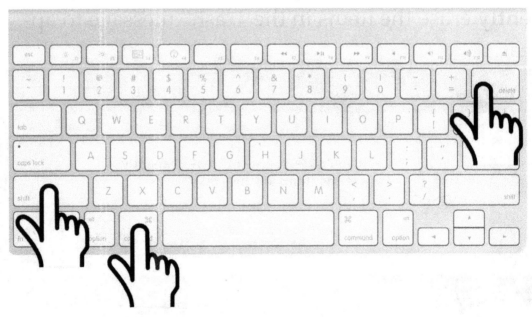

empty trash keyboard shortcut

retrieve file from trash

1) Open your Mac's Trash can by clicking on it one time:

2) When the Trash window opens, you can "control-click" on the file that you wish to retrieve:

3) Select "Put Back" from the pop-up menu:

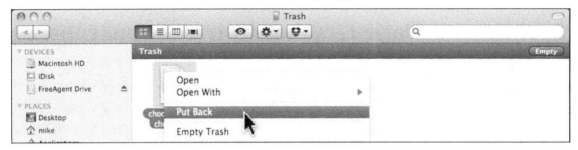

This will send the **file** back to the **folder** (or storage location) it was in when you deleted it.

You can also *click & drag* an item out of the Trash window (circled below):

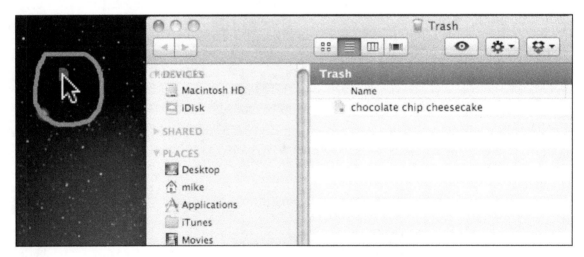

file being "dragged" out of window

THE SYSTEM PREFERENCES WINDOW

You can open the "System Preferences" window either by clicking its icon on your program dock:

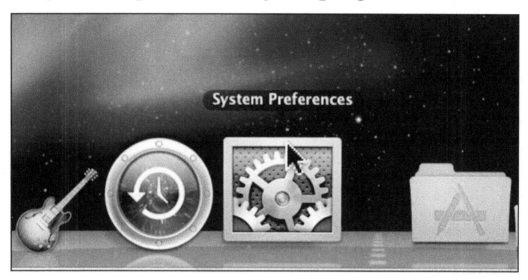

Or by selecting *System Preferences* from the menu:

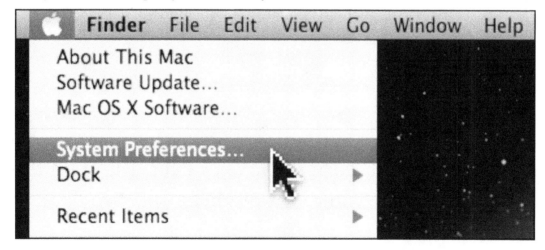

desktop picture

You can change your Mac's desktop picture by first using the mouse to click the "Desktop & Screen Saver" button (circled below):

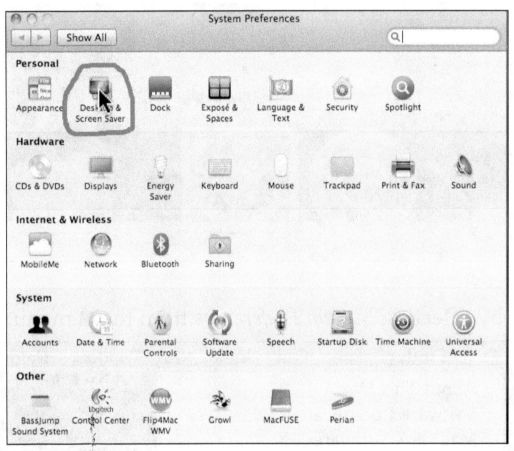

Please *single-click* everything on the System Preferences window.

You can click a folder on the left side of the window...

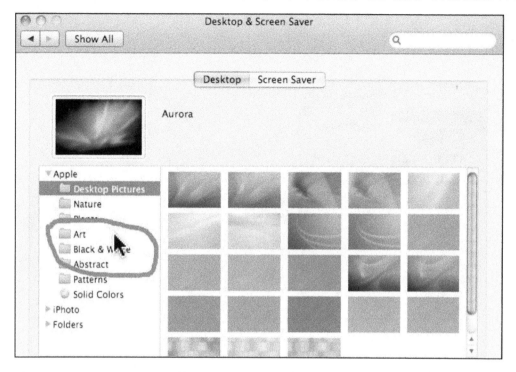

... to display the contents of that folder on the **right side** of the window:

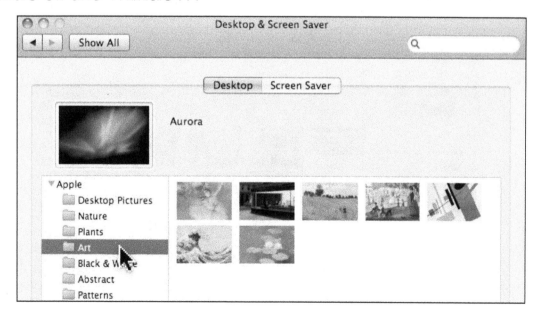

Simply click on a picture to select it for your desktop:

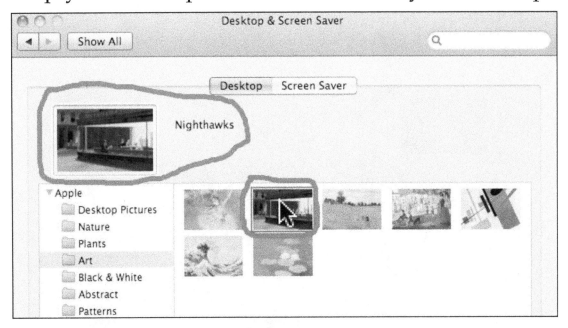

You can also select a photo from your iPhoto library:

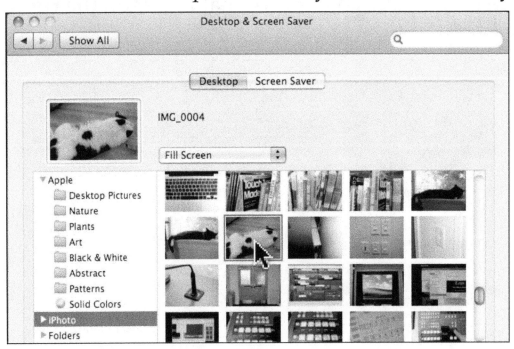

screen saver

1) Click the "Screen Saver" tab near the top of the window (circled below):

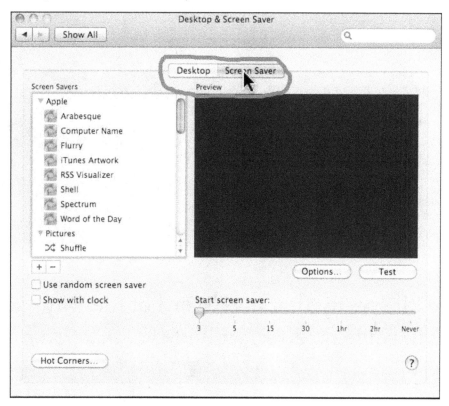

2) If necessary, click the little arrow on the left side of "Apple" (circled below):

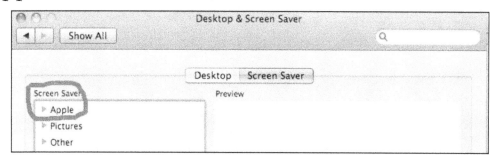

3) Select a screen saver:

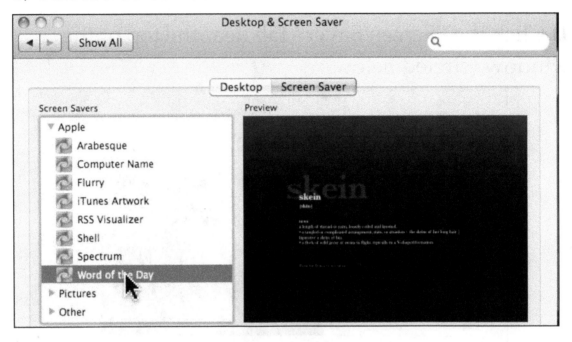

4) Here I'll specify that my "Word of the Day" screen saver will come on after 5 minutes of *inactivity*:

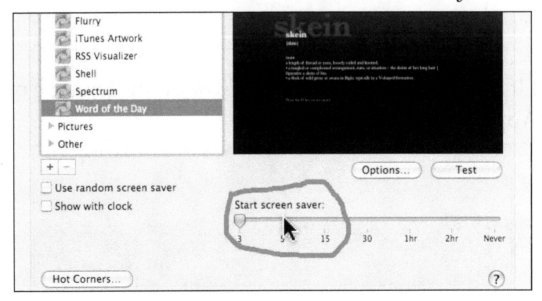

5) You can click the *Test* button (underneath the screen saver "preview" area) to see how your selected screen saver will look (full screen):

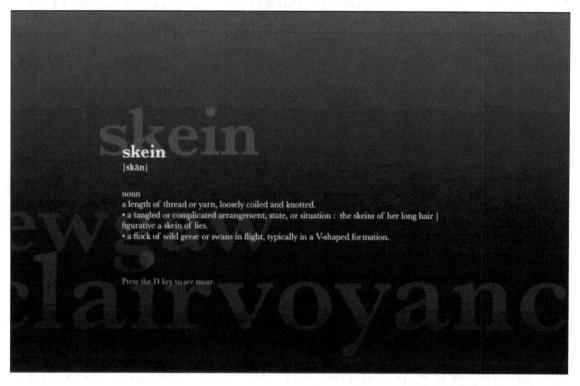

(Press any key on your keyboard to make the screen saver test / preview go away.)

I'll also check the "Show with clock" checkbox:

navigation

Like the Finder window, the **System Preferences** window has "back" and "forward" buttons that you can use to *retrace* or *move forward* in your window browsing history.

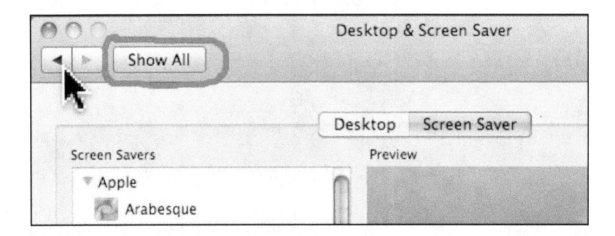

You can click the "Show All" button (circled above) to quickly return to the System Preferences main window.

energy saver

You can cut down on your energy bill (and help preserve the life of your Mac's display) by specifying "Computer sleep" and/or "Display sleep".

Click the "Energy Saver" button on the second row:

This will cause the "Energy Saver" window to open:

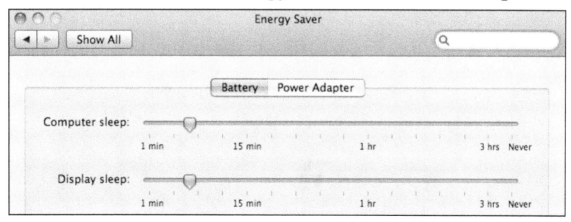

Both of your "computer sleep" and "display sleep" times have to be **later** than your **screen saver** time (if you set one).

Keeping in mind that my screen saver is set for **5 minutes**, I'll specify that if I don't use my Mac for **15 minutes**, both the computer and the display should into "sleep" mode (which is a low-energy using state).

You can press and hold down the mouse button to move the slider button:

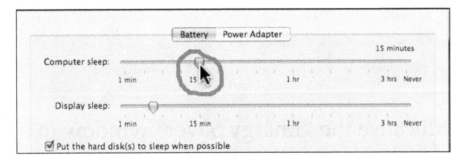

Or *click* your preferred time on the timeline:

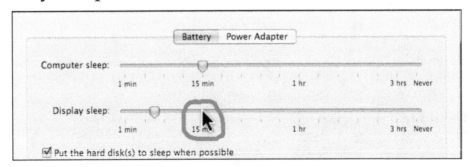

The energy saver preferences *checkboxes* (circled below) were already checked (by Apple) so I've never unchecked mine:

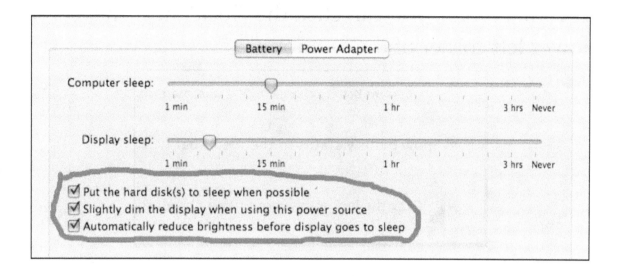

You can quickly wake your Mac up from *sleep* mode by pressing any key on your computer keyboard and/or by clicking the mouse.

click the lock to prevent further changes

If you want to lock (or unlock) your *system preferences* (for the section that you are currently in as well as several others), you can click the "lock" near the lower left corner of the window:

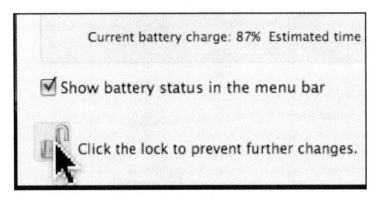

If you "unlock" the lock (so that you *can* make changes), you'll be directed to type in your Mac's administrator password:

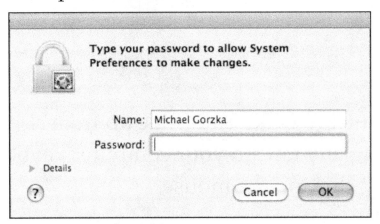

My **admin** password is my oldest cat's name followed by the year of my Dad's birth (no spaces).

Trackpad

If you have a MacBook, you can adjust how the built-in mouse works by clicking the "Trackpad" button (located on the **Hardware** row):

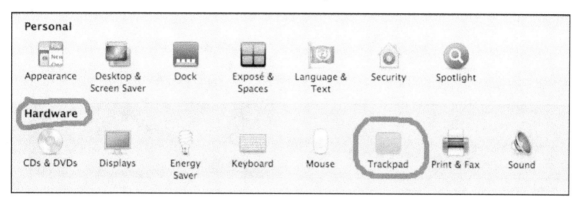

If you don't care to hold down the "control" key on your keyboard (as you click the mouse) to cause a **pop-up menu** to appear...

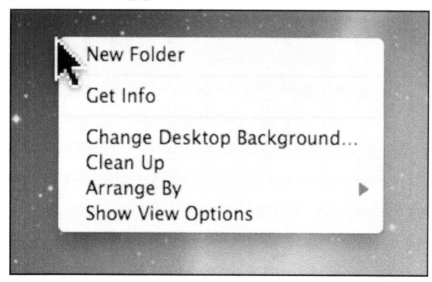

You can instead click the *Secondary Click* checkbox...

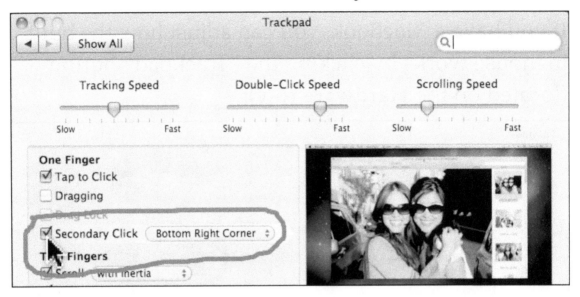

...which will (by default) enable you to press the **lower right corner** of the touchpad when you want a pop-up menu:

There are numerous other settings you can adjust but personally I think they're all more trouble than they're worth (but feel free to experiment with them as you can't break anything).

screen cursor size

You can change your screen arrow (or *cursor*) from its default *teeny-tiny* size to a significantly larger size through your Mac's "Universal Access" settings:

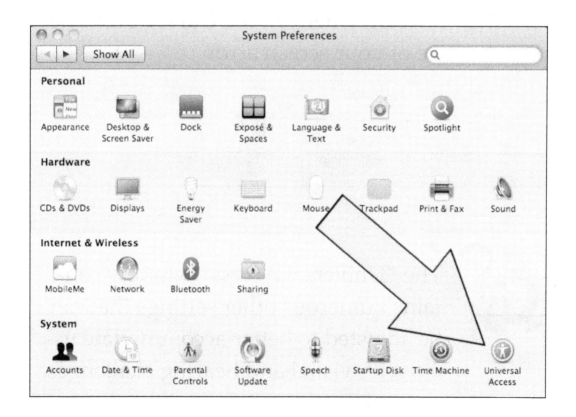

Click that button and (if necessary) select the "Mouse & Trackpad" button:

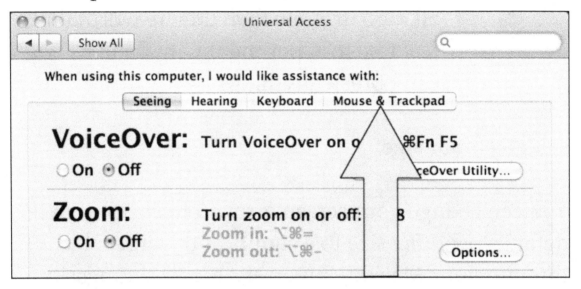

You can then click anywhere on the **Cursor Size** line to adjust the size of your screen arrow:

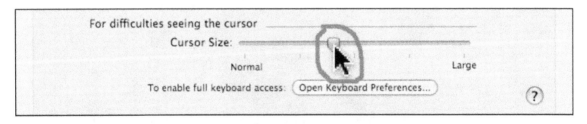

 The "Universal Access" window contains numerous other settings that can be adjusted to better accommodate users with visual and hearing challenges.

DOCK TRICKS

hide the program dock

If you would like some more screen real estate (or if you find its constant presence to be a distraction), you can "hide" the program dock.

1) Place the tip of the screen arrow directly over "Dock" on the menu:

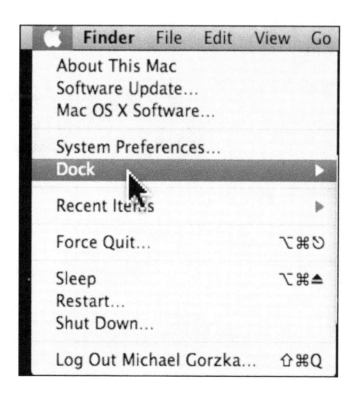

This will cause the "Dock" menu to appear:

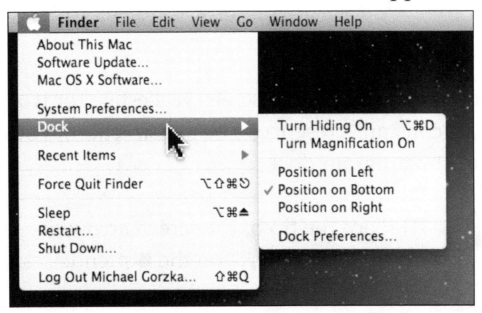

Here we'll select both "Turn Hiding On" and "Turn Magnification On":

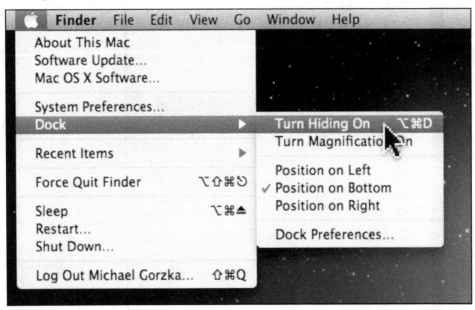

Before menu selections:

(I've enlarged the screen arrow so you can see it better. Please note the Safari icon is **not** magnified.)

After menu selections:

(Now the program dock will automatically pop-up and magnify when you put your screen arrow any-where over it.)

Here I've used the "Dock" menu to put the program dock on the **side** of my Mac computer screen:

(*Cyberduck* by the way, is a righteous and well-regarded "donationware" FTP program --- used to upload files from my Mac to my various websites.)

Your author keeps his dock on the **bottom** of his screen with **hiding** and **magnification** turned on --- as he finds the program dock to be a bit *distracting* and the magnification effect to be quite cool.

ADMINISTRATION PANEL

As we'll see in the next chapter, you'll need your Mac's administrator *password* to keep your Mac up to date for Apple software, system and security **updates**.

To access your Mac's Administrator panel, first open the System Preferences window.

Click the **Accounts** button on the "System" row:

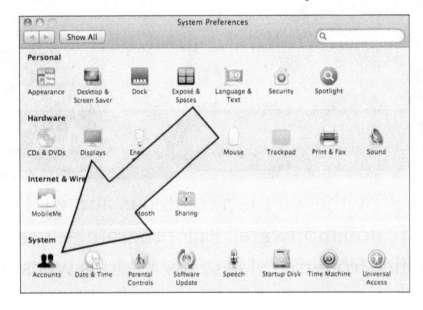

TIP: You can also type "Accounts" into the Spotlight search box for quicker access:

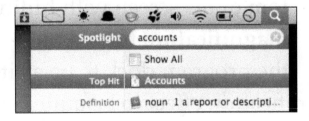

You can use the *Accounts* screen to accomplish numerous administrative tasks:

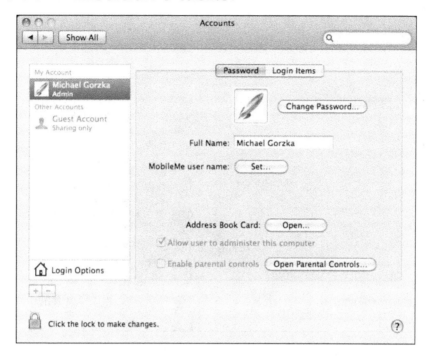

You can change your Administrator *picture* by first clicking on it one time (circled below):

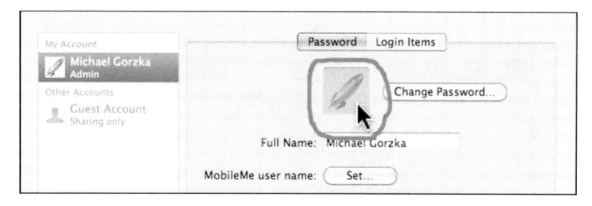

You can then select a picture (one that suits you better) from the drop-down menu:

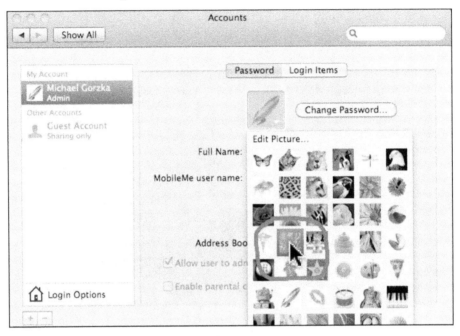

address book card

Here is the picture that I just selected on my Address Book card:

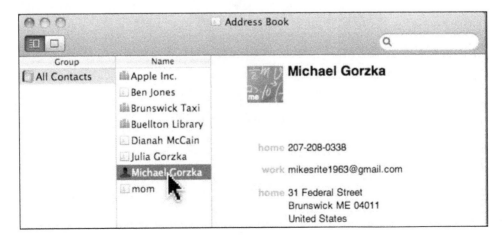

Login Items

Would you like a particular program to *automatically start* when you turn your Mac on (or restart it)?

1) If so, click the "Login Items" tab:

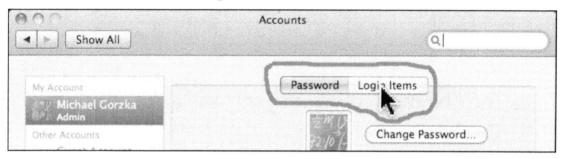

2) Click the *plus sign* near the bottom of the window:

This will cause your *Applications* folder to "drop down":

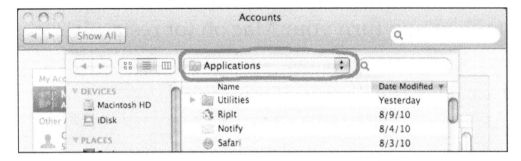

Click the "Name" column to *sort* the applications:

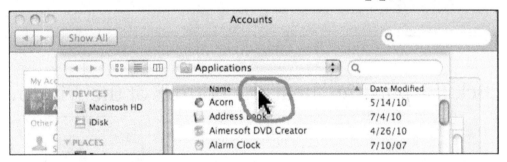

Scroll down the window and select the application that you want to automatically open:

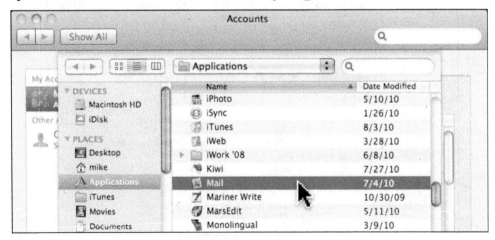

And click the "Add" button (circled below):

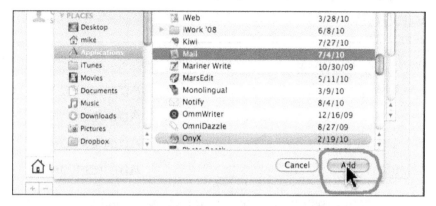

This will place the selected item in the list of "Login Items":

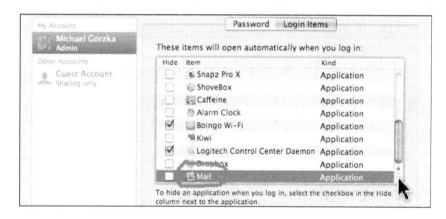

You can *remove* an application from this list by clicking on it one time (to select it):

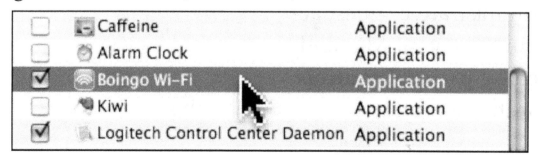

And then by clicking the minus sign near the bottom of the window:

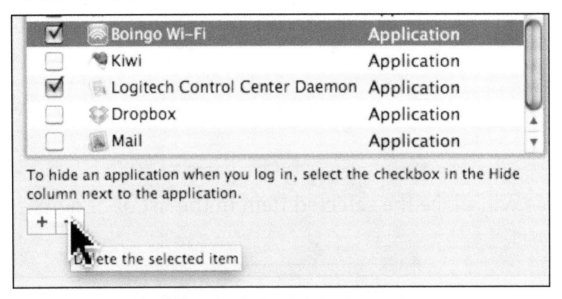

(I rarely fly these days so I don't need the Boingo Wi-Fi always running in the background. I can always start the application "manually" if I need it.)

attention parents!

Please visit www.mac-shy.com for a free video tutorial on creating a non-administrative "guest account" on your Mac and setting **parental controls** for that account.

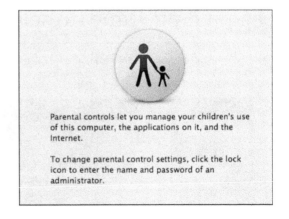

SOFTWARE UPDATES

When Apple releases software, security, and system **updates** for your Mac, a software update screen will automatically appear:

You can "manually" check to see if any updates are available for your Mac by selecting *Software Update* from the menu:

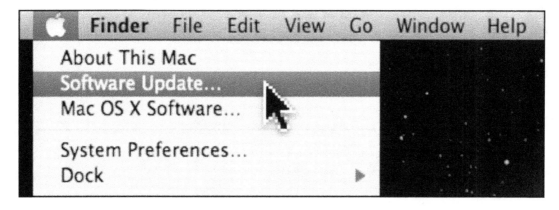

If updates *are* available, you can download and install them by clicking the "Continue" button or by pressing the **return** key on your keyboard:

Before you click "Continue" (or press the **return** key), you can click the "Show Details" button:

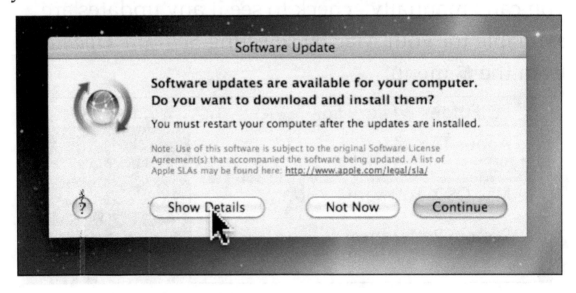

You can then *single-click* any of the updates to learn more about it (including its file size and if it will require a **restart**):

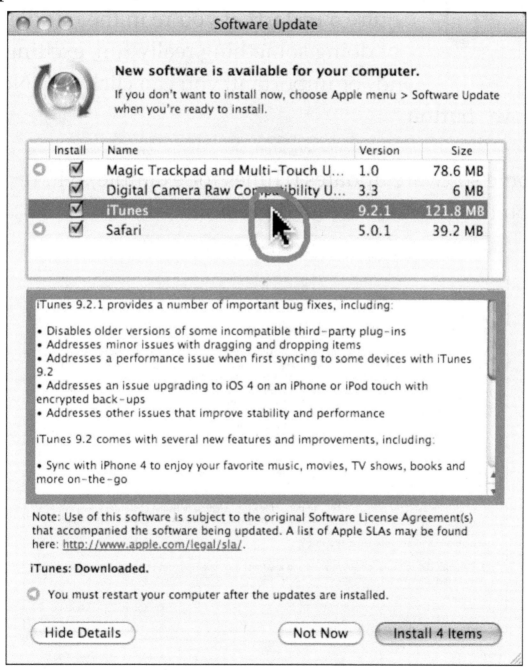

Downloading and installing updates can slow down your Mac (as well as require a **restart**), if you're in the middle of doing something really fun, exciting and/or important, you can click the "Not Now" button.

Some software updates (iTunes for example) will re you to agree to a *License Agreement*:

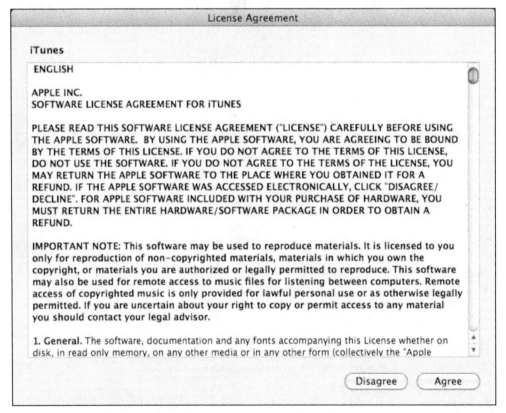

Since the "Agree" button at the lower right corner of the agreement is not highlighted, you'll have to click it with the mouse.

After you agree to any license agreements, the updates will "download" to your Mac:

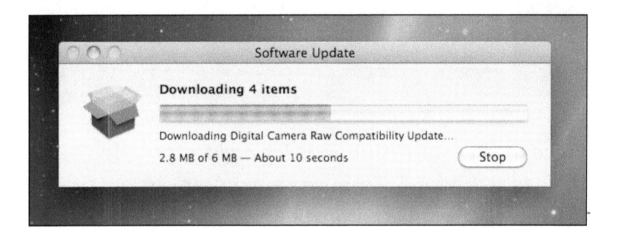

This may some time depending on the **file size** of the updates and the **speed** of your Internet connection.

If you have a MacBook, Apple strongly suggests that it be plugged into a power source while you are downloading and installing updates.

After the updates have finished *downloading* from Apple HQ to your Mac, a "Restart" window may appear:

Since the "Restart" button is *highlighted,* you don't have to reach for the mouse —- you can simply press the **return** key on your keyboard.

Again if you're in the middle of something, you can click the "Not Now" button and the updates that you downloaded will be **installed** after you restart your Mac.

Depending on the updates, you may also have to type in your Mac's Administrator password (which you chose when you first set up your Mac).

lost your admin password?

If you don't know your administrator password, it *may be* nada, niente, zip, zilch, zero, bupkis.

In other words, try clicking the **OK** button while leaving the password field *blank*:

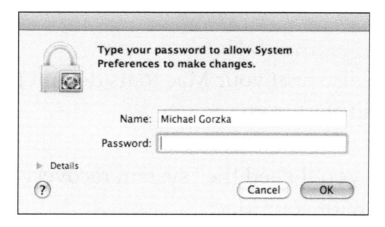

If your password isn't blank:

You have two options to reset it:

1) You can call your nearest Apple store (or authorized service provider) and tell them that you need help resetting your Admin password.

2) You can also *reset* your Mac to its default factory settings and start from scratch.

To do this, you'll need the "system recovery" discs that came with your Mac:

This procedure will **erase** all your files, documents, photos, music, videos, downloaded programs, et al.

In short, you'll lose everything!

In order to keep this book to a manageable length, I've created a mini-instructional *video* for re-installing your Mac's operating system (or OS) and put it online:

www.mac-shy.com

If you don't have *high speed internet*, please visit a friend who does or pay a call on your local public library.

HOW TO SURF THE WEB WITH SAFARI

You can start the Safari web browser by clicking its icon on the program dock:

You can highlight the current web address (which by default will be the Apple Start page) by holding down one of the "command" keys on your keyboard as you press the letter "L" key:

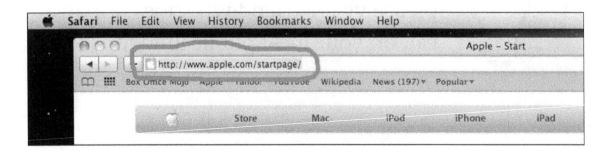

 You can also use the mouse to click inside the web address **three times** in quick succession: *knock knock knock*:

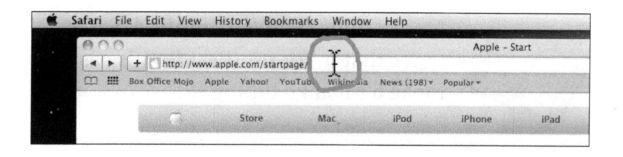

After the current web address has been highlighted, you can type the web address of the web site that you wish to visit:

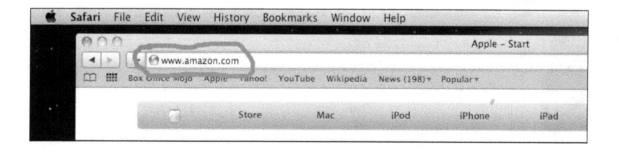

Double-check it for accuracy and press the "return" key on your keyboard.

Do we need to type in **http://** at the beginning of the web address?

No we don't, *http://* is **implied**. Safari types that in for us. (Besides it's easy to make a mistake typing it.)

back & forward

You can click the "back" button to *return* to the web page you were most previously on:

And conversely, you can click the "forward" button to (you guessed it!) move **forward** in your web browsing history:

tabs

You can have *multiple* web pages open (at the same time) **within the same Safari window** by using "tabs".

You can select "New Tab" from the Safari **File** menu:

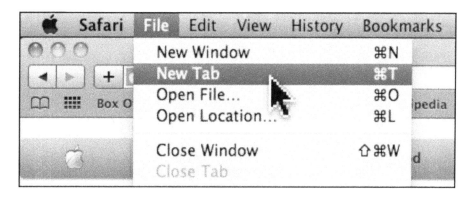

But it's much faster to use the "command + t" keyboard shortcut:

After a new tab has been opened, the *blinking line* will be in the **web address box** for that tab:

This being the case, you can type in the web address of the web site (or web **page**) that you wish to visit...

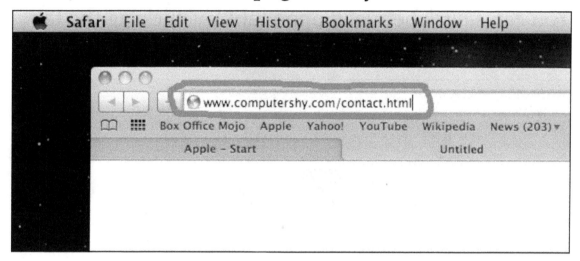

...and press the "return" key on your keyboard:

switch between open tabs

You can *switch* between open tabs by clicking the tab that you want to view (circled below):

close tabs

You can close a tab (and the web page it contains) by clicking the tab's **close** button (circled below):

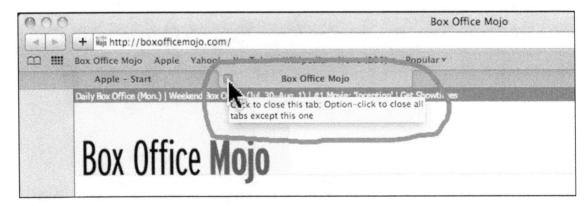

You can also select "Close Tab" from the Safari **File** menu to close the tab that you currently have open:

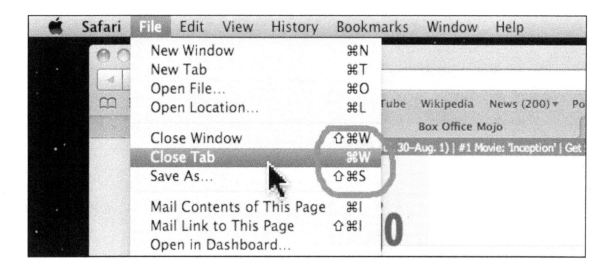

(Please note the corresponding "command - w" key-board shortcut on that menu selection.)

"option click"

Right now I have 8 web page tabs open:

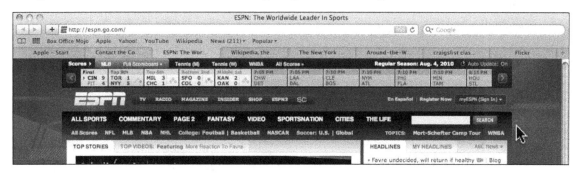

If you hold down the **option** key on your keyboard as you click a tab's "close" button...

...all the open tabs will close *except* the tab whose close button you just "option-clicked":

web search

If you don't know the web **address** of a web site that you wish to visit or if you want *information* on a particular subject, you can use the **search box** which is at the top right corner of the Safari window.

You can use the mouse to click anywhere inside the search box…

…to put the "blinking line" in there:

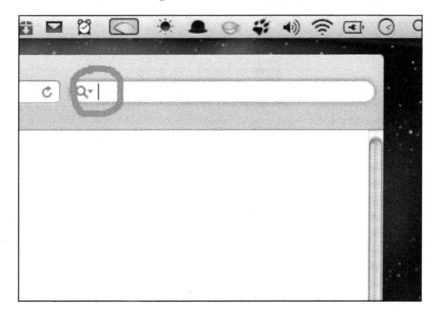

Type in what you are looking for:

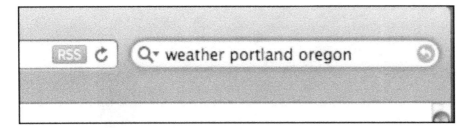

And press the "return" key on your keyboard.

This will take you to a Google search results page for whatever you typed into the search box:

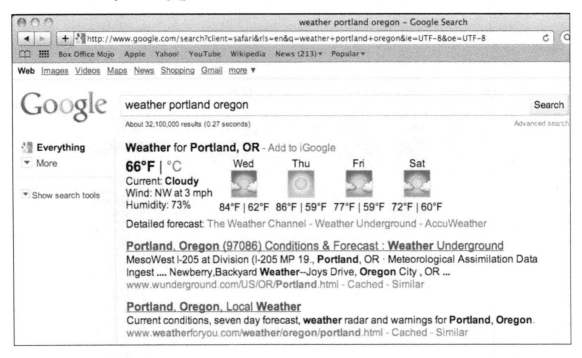

You can "click" on a search result link by using the mouse to place the tip of your screen arrow directly over it (circled below):

Portland, Oregon, Local Weather
Current conditions, five day forecast, **weather** radar and warnings for **Portland, Oregon**.
www.weatherforyou.com/weather/oregon/portland.html - Cached - Similar

Hold the mouse very still and click the mouse one time.

This will take you the **web page** that the *link* leads to:

Remember you can click the "back" button to return to the web page that you were most previously on:

web page scrolling

You can *scroll* up and down a Safari window either by "clicking & dragging" the window *scroll bar*:

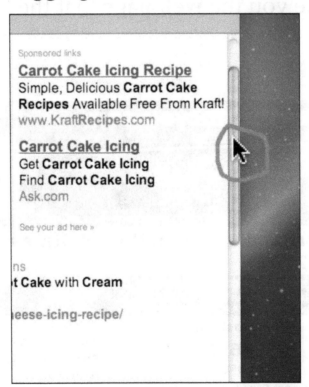

Or by pressing the "arrow keys" on your keyboard.

You may have to click on a **blank area** of the web page (circled below) to be able to **scroll** the web page by pressing the keyboard arrow keys.

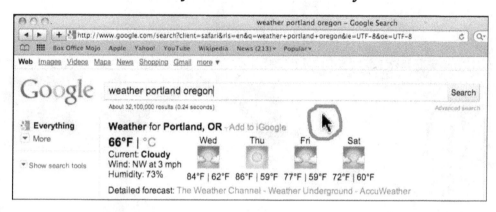

You can scroll down a web page in *bigger chunks* by pressing your keyboard's spacebar:

APPLE MAIL SETUP

You can *connect* your web based **email** account (i.e. Hotmail, Yahoo, Gmail, et al.) to the "Mail" program on your Mac.

Why would you want to do this?

- ✓ Attaching photos, documents, zip files, etc. is much easier
- ✓ Immediate notification of new email messages
- ✓ Instant access to your email (you don't have to go to a web site and "sign in")
- ✓ Mail integrates easily with iCal, Address Book, Photo Booth and iPhoto

The "Mail" application rates a book of its own (which is why I've written one and created a video program for it) so in this book we'll briefly explain how you can access your email through **Mail**.

Start the Mail program by clicking its program dock icon:

You can also start **Mail** from within your "Applications" folder or by typing "mail" into the *Spotlight* search box (both as previously described.)

The first time you start **Mail** (or until you connect it to an email account), a "Welcome to Mail" screen will appear:

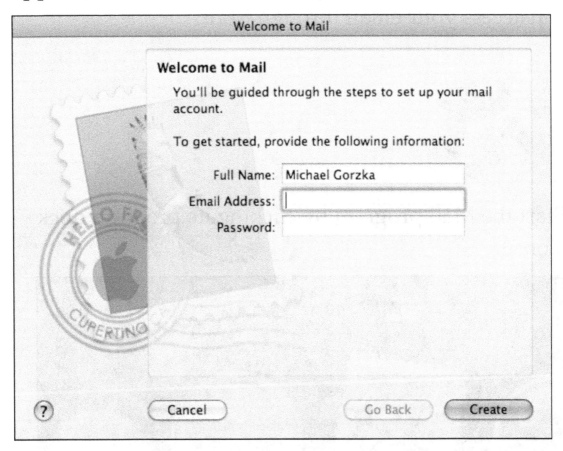

(The Mail program will pull your "Full Name" from your Mac's Administrator account.)

1) If you want to use a different name for your email (perhaps just your first name or a nickname), you can

delete what is currently in the name box and type in something different:

2) Type your email address into the "Email Address" box:

Please double-check your email address to make sure it's correct (as there's no margin of error here).

3) Press the "Tab" key on your keyboard and type in your email password:

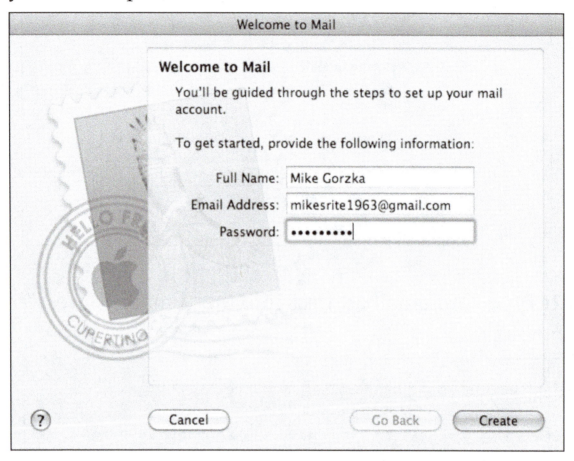

(You won't be able to see what you are typing into a password box so you have to be extra careful here.)

4) Next (as the "Create" button is highlighted), you can press the "return" key on your computer keyboard.

When you're working on any kind of a **form** on a computer, never press the **return** key on your keyboard *until* you have completed the form.

If you typed your email address and password in correctly (and your Mac is connected to the Internet), your **Mail** *Inbox* will open:

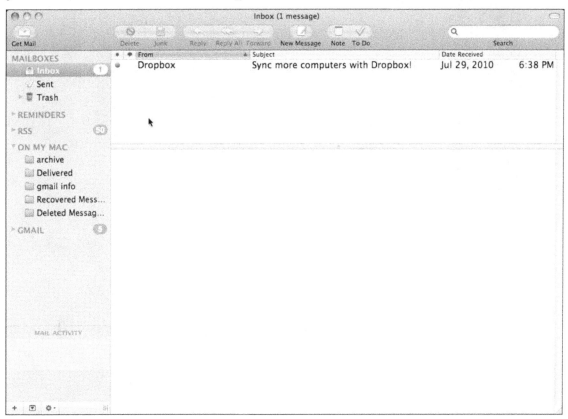

You can make your Mail icons bigger by clicking the **View** menu and *deselecting* "Use Small Mailbox Icons":

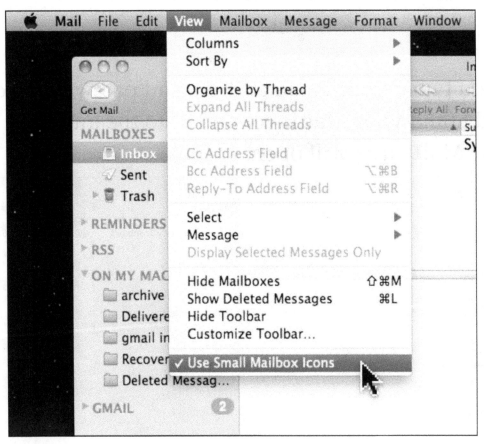

For more information on the Apple Mail program, please go to www.mac-shy.com.

HOW TO ATTACH A PRINTER

Due to the *ease* that documents can be emailed and photos can be uploaded to websites like Flickr, there are many less reasons to waste ink and kill trees.

That being said, you can easily attach any USB printer to your Mac:

USB stands for "Universal Serial Bus" but for our purposes, it really means "plug and play".

As we'll see, there's very little (if any) configuration involved and you probably won't have to install any software that came with the printer that you bought.

How do I know if a printer is *USB* or not?

Most (if not all) of the printers you can buy from CompUSA, Best Buy, Apple, et al. will be USB.

If you're not sure if a printer is compatible with your Mac, please ask a sales associate.

But your **MacBook**, **iMac**, or **Mac mini** should automatically recognize (and be able to print to) any USB printer that you attach to it.

1) Carefully unpack your printer and assemble it (as per the instructions that came with it).

2) Carefully plug the smaller end of the printer's USB cable into the printer:

3) Plug the larger end of the cable into one of the USB "ports" on your Mac:

 I'm using my MacBook for demonstration purposes but the procedure will be just the same for an iMac or Mac mini.

USB openings or "ports" are marked by a pitchfork-like symbol.

4) Put paper in your printer and power it on:

5) Start the "TextEdit" program (as previously described) and create a test document:

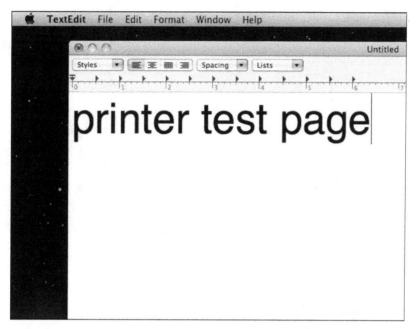

6) You can then select "Print" from the TextEdit **File** menu:

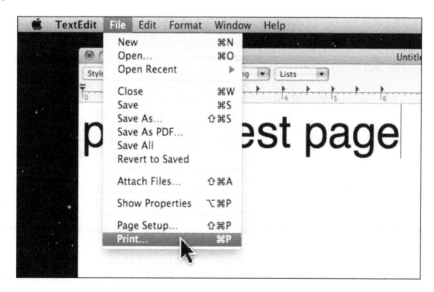

You can also use the *command - p* keyboard shortcut:

Make sure your printer is in the **Printer** box (circled below):

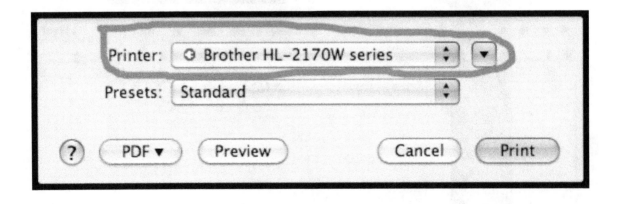

And click the "Print" button (or simply press your keyboard's "return" key).

Your test document should then print:

HOW TO CONNECT TO THE INTERNET

Newer Mac computers come equipped with a built-in "Airport" card.

This means that you can connect to the Internet without any wires.

If your house / apartment building / coffee shop / public library has a wireless network (i.e. "wi-fi"), you can follow this procedure to connect to it:

Use the mouse to click the "Airport" icon near the top right corner of your Mac computer computer screen (it looks like an upside down triangle).

If necessary, select "Turn Airport On" from the pull-down menu:

(Wait a few moments for the AirPort card inside your Mac to activate.)

Select the wireless network that you wish to connect to:

The "lock" adjacent to a wireless network indicates that you must have a *username* and a *password* in order to connect to the Internet through that network.

(Some apartment buildings offer free Internet and supply their tenants with usernames and passwords.)

What do I need to do in order to create my own wireless network?

We cover this subject in detail in "How to set up a Mac Network: a step-by-step guide for the mac computer shy".

But for right now, the **easiest** way to set up a home network is to purchase a *wireless router* from your local computer store (or buy one online) and then order high speed cable internet.

Ask the technician to attach the cable modem (which they will provide) to your wireless router.

NOTE: Apple sells wireless routers but there are cheaper alternatives that will work just as well.

Do I need to connect my Mac to the Internet through Airport?

No, you have the option to connect wirelessly but you don't have to.

Simply ask the cable guy to attach your Mac directly to the cable modem:

 When ordering Internet service, tell the customer service representative that you have a *Mac* computer.

Also tell them how you plan to connect to the Internet.

Please visit www.mac-shy.com for more information on Mac computer networks --- such as how to secure them!

11 TIPS FOR USING YOUR NEW MAC

1) Stay neat & organized (don't liter your desktop).

2) If you're experienced with using a Windows PC, don't get psyched out!

Yes, the Mac environment looks a bit different.

But please keep in mind that Mac computers and Windows computers do pretty much the same things and work pretty much the same way.

3) Use the Mac keyboard shortcuts & don't double-click the mouse unnecessarily.

4) Use the "command - tab" keyboard shortcut to switch between programs that you have open.

5) Remember you can "control-click" the mouse to cause a pop-up (or a "context") menu to appear.

6) Look at the top left corner of your Mac computer screen to see which program is currently "active" (or has context).

7) Remember that clicking *anywhere* on a blank area of the desktop will make "Finder" the active program.

8) When you switch to a different application, use the "Hide Others" menu selection (or its *option-command-h* keyboard shortcut).

9) Remember you can start an application from the program dock; from within the Applications folder; or by using *Spotlight*.

10) Remember you can quickly open a **Finder** window by clicking the Finder icon on the far left side of the program dock.

11) Keep in mind that the **active** window will have colorful buttons (red, yellow, & green).

You can visit www.mac-shy.com for additional tips, tutorials, and instructional videos.

www.ingramcontent.com/pod-product-compliance
Lightning Source LLC
Chambersburg PA
CBHW080409060326
40689CB00019B/4179